JANE'S RAILWAY YEAR

EDITED BY MURRAY BROWN

JANE'S

Copyright © Jane's Publishing Company
Limited 1982

First published in the United Kingdom in
1982 by
Jane's Publishing Company Limited
238 City Road, London EC1V 2PU

ISBN 0 7106 0189 1

Designed by Bernard Crossland
Associates

Printed in Great Britain by
Netherwood Dalton & Co Ltd
Huddersfield

COVER PHOTOGRAPHS

Front
The eagerly awaited return to steam of Frank
Beaumont's ex-S&DJR 7F 2-8-0 No 13809
occurred on 2 May 1981. This fine machine is
seen pounding out of York on the return leg of
this first run. *(Murray Brown)*

Rear
Woodhead's final winter is recalled in this picture of two class 76s descending past Thurlestone with loaded HAA hoppers in February
1981. *(Les Nixon)*

TITLE PAGE
Made redundant by the closure of the
Woodhead route, Nos 76015 and 76040 for-
lornly await their fate at Reddish on 13 September. *(Tom Heavyside)*

On 26 July 1981 Sunday and Bank Holiday passenger services began on the Llangollen Railway's
half mile stretch of line from Llangollen towards Corwen. The only standard gauge steam operated
railway in North Wales, the line is managed by the Llangollen Railway Society Ltd, which leases
from Clwyd County Council and Glyndwr District Council the ten mile trackbed of the former
GWR route to Corwen. The railway's Kitson-built 0-6-0ST of 1932 was photographed returning to
Llangollen station with the inaugural 'Burtonwood Brewer' on 26 July. See also our 'Open for
business' feature on p99. *(Ray Hughes, Llangollen Railway Society Ltd)*

More regular incursions into South Wales by LMR-based class 40s have led to their employment on
certain WR domestic duties, notably turns from Severn Tunnel Junction to Exeter and Llandeilo
Junction. As a result some crews at Severn Tunnel Junction have 'learnt' locomotives of this type. In
this view taken at the depot on 17 December Inspector D Flood (left) explains to Drivers Collett and
Evans the finer points of No 40009. Also visible in the picture are Nos 40087 (left) and 40136. *(Derek
Short)*

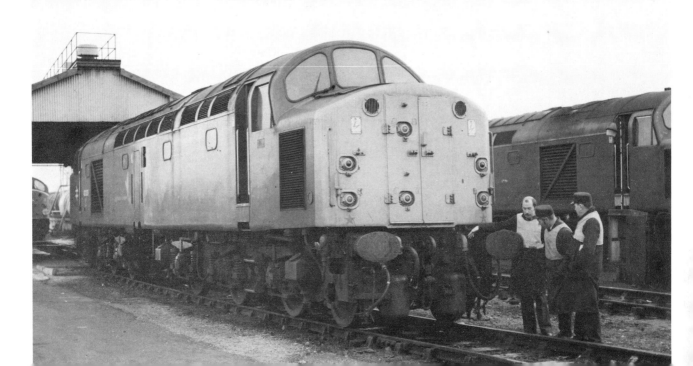

INTRODUCTION

Welcome to this first edition of *Jane's Railway Year*. In the pages which follow we portray in pictures the major news stories and developments affecting Britain's railways in 1981.

Observers of our constantly changing national railway scene can find around them a wealth of activity to absorb their interest, as a review of any year will show. A retrospective glance reveals that 1981 is no exception and our introductory commentaries to each of the sections listed opposite pick out the high (and low) spots during the enthusiast's year. These are, of course, featured in detail. At the same time we have endeavoured to bring to the reader's attention some of the apparently less significant events which nonetheless reflect the nature of both the national system and private railways during the period under review.

Our picture report on British Rail during 1981 places particular emphasis on the changing structure and deployment of the locomotive and rolling stock fleet. However, we also focus attention on the constant evolution of BR's network and infrastructure with reports on electrification progress, improved passenger facilities, system rationalisation and many other aspects of the changing fabric of the railway. Features depicting some of the trends in the pattern of BR passenger and freight traffic conclude our review of BR in 1981.

Followers of steam and the world of railway preservation will find extensive coverage of their highlights of 1981, including a striking pictorial survey of the year's more notable steam-hauled railtours.

In a year marked by the frustrating circumstances surrounding the public debut of APT-P, the *de facto* end of the Deltics and the closure of the electrified Woodhead route, there has been much to report and record. Our review extends far beyond these to embrace new rolling stock, resignalling schemes, vintage carriage preservation and a host of other detailed items which all deserve mention. If in the magnitude of this task we have omitted a topic of particular importance to any reader, an apology is tendered.

MURRAY BROWN

Harrogate
December 1981

ACKNOWLEDGEMENTS

This book has only been possible with the generous help and enthusiasm of our contributors, many of whom went to extraordinary lengths to obtain our pictures. They are credited individually in each picture caption but to them all the editor and publishers extend their grateful thanks. In addition we gratefully acknowledge the assistance of BR staff at the Regional Public Relations Officer's Departments at Euston, Glasgow, Paddington, Waterloo and York, Divisional PROs at Bristol, Cardiff and Preston, Public Relations staff at BREL, Derby, and the Press Office personnel at Freightliners Ltd. It is our pleasure to thank them for their interest and valued help in contributing to this record of a memorable railway year.

Photographic contributions

We are pleased to receive photographic contributions for consideration for the next edition of *Jane's Railway Year*. Suitable black and white prints or colour transparencies of subjects appropriate to 1982 should be packed securely and sent to:

The Editor
Jane's Railway Year
238 City Road
London EC1V 2PU

CONTENTS

BR MOTIVE POWER AND ROLLING STOCK

Although for BR the traction highlight of 1981 was no doubt the short lived entry into revenue service of APT-P, the year for enthusiasts was dominated by the rapid run-down of the incomparable Deltics. Only BR's melancholy finale on 2 January 1982 prevents us recording the last chapter in the career of this remarkable class.

Hopes for passenger services of a more local and rural nature were raised during the year by the appearance of the unglamorous but functional class 140 two-car diesel mechanical trainset and the BRE-Leyland railbus.

Stock for the St Pancras-Bedford Midland Suburban Electrification in the shape of the new generation class 317 emus started to arrive at Cricklewood in October, while GE line inner suburban services benefitted from full scale introduction of the class 315 units.

ER HSTs extended their field of operation to Tees-side, north Humberside and Glasgow. More significantly, from 5 October recently delivered WR sets were deployed on certain services on the North-East/South-West axis.

Deliveries of class 56 freight locomotives continued from BREL Doncaster during 1981, examples being sent to Healey Mills and Tinsley depots.

Our features on SR and GE emu refurbishment serve to demonstrate that this activity remains a keynote of BR's policy of improving facilities for suburban travellers within continued investment constraints.

For the enthusiast, however, the gains rarely match the losses, and 1981 witnessed the withdrawal from capital stock of the MSW class 76s, the last class 31/0 "Toffee-apple" and Scotland's home-grown class 06 shunters, although examples of the first two types happily are preserved for future curiosity. Obsolesence and the recession also conspired to reduce the ranks of classes 25, 40, 45 and 46, many examples of these types finding their way to Swindon to await their fate.

The class 306 emus, veterans from the 1949 Liverpool Street-Shenfield electrification, passed from the passenger scene in October, while on the Southern more 4-SUBs were retired.

In the field of hauled passenger stock, the well appointed Mk 3 sleeping car made its important debut during 1981, first deliveries being for East Coast services.

Development of BR's Speedlink network of fast air-braked freight services continues to stimulate new wagon designs and 1981 witnessed the appearance of several new types. At the same time the economic climate has hastened the move away from the traditional British short wheelbase wagon and many, especially the unfitted variety, have been scrapped. BR's withdrawal from C & D parcels traffic during 1981 also led to a considerable reduction in the numbers of pre-nationalisation vans, making vehicles of this type quite a rarity.

One frequent working for the Deltics in their final months of service was the 0850 York-Liverpool Lime Street and the 1305 return. Latterly these trains were particularly used to test the four members of the class rostered to operate the programme of farewell tours, trial runs usually being made midweek prior to the following weekend's tours. Such was the case when No 55015 *Tulyar* was photographed at Diggle on 2 December with the 1305 from Liverpool. *(Les Nixon)*

A beautifully groomed No 55007 *Pinza* waits for the 'off' from Kings Cross with the last locomotive-hauled 1705 to Hull on 3 January 1981. As this date was a Saturday, the headboard was not strictly accurate, 'The Hull Executive' being only so titled Mondays-Fridays. However, the timings were similar and no complaint was heard from the enthusiast community! From the 5 January, this train became a HST working. It had been the intention to use No 55003 *Meld* as this locomotive had worked the very first 'The Hull Executive'—one of the all time legendary Deltic runs—and it was hoped to emulate this memorable performance. Sadly, No 55003 was withdrawn on 31 December 1980 thus thwarting the plan. Nevertheless, Finsbury Park had provided another of their favourites, No 55007, and the locomotive carried the unofficial headboard manufactured by one of the staff at Finsbury Park. *(John Chalcraft)*

Deltic twilight

The decision taken in the summer of 1981 to bring forward withdrawal of the class 55s from May to January 1982 ensured that 1981 would be the swan song year of this legendary design, with BR enterprise and enthusiast efforts joining forces to stage a fitting end for a remarkable locomotive type.

The Deltic Preservation Society with the co-operation of BR Eastern Region celebrated twenty years of Deltic service on 28 February 1981 with a special headboard on the 1220 Kings Cross-York. No 55022 *Royal Scots Grey* was specially selected for this train as it was 20 years to the day since it entered service. The driver, Mr George Craven of Huntingdon, York, joined in a celebratory glass on arrival at York and the intercom on the train was used to good effect en route with passengers made well aware of the significance of their train. The 1220 is seen here north of Potters Bar in atrocious weather. *(Ken Harris)*

The anniversary headboard on Deltic 55022 at York. *(Murray Brown)*

Since being chosen by the National Railway Museum as its future Deltic, No 55002, now resplendent in its original two-tone green livery, inevitably has been nominated for various special trains. One such occasion was 4 May 1981 when it hauled a BR sponsored special, the 'Deltic Fenman', from Kings Cross to the Nene Valley Railway. After depositing its Mk 1 coaches, the Deltic delighted photographers by hauling a rake of continental stock and is seen here leaving Orton Mere for Wansford. *(Tom Heavyside)*

To commemorate 55015's participation in the Rainhill Cavalcade on 24-26 May 1980, BR kindly consented to permitting the Deltic Preservation Society to provide at its own expense a plaque. Neville Davies, Divisional Maintenance Engineer, Kings Cross unveils the plaque on *Tulyar* on 17 March. Also in attendance are Allan Baker, Depot Manager (centre), whilst on the left is DPS Chairman, David Carter. *(Roger Newling-Goode)*

ROCKET 150
THIS LOCOMOTIVE RAN IN THE LIVERPOOL & MANCHESTER RAILWAY 150TH ANNIVERSARY CAVALCADE AT RAINHILL 24-25-26 MAY 1980

THIS PLAQUE PRESENTED BY THE DELTIC PRESERVATION SOCIETY

A close-up of the plaque fitted to each end of No 55015. *(Roger Newling-Goode)*

To mark the end of Finsbury Park as a maintenance depot on 31 May 1981, Deltic 55009 *Alycidon* was specially groomed to work the 1605 Kings Cross-York. Stuart Whitter (left), Rolling Stock and Plant Engineer at March, who provided the commemorative headboard, shakes hands with Allan Baker, Depot Manager, Finsbury Park, both men accompanying the Deltic in the cab from London. The headboard was removed at Doncaster where the photograph was taken. No 55009 also carried a wreath. Stuart, when based at Finsbury Park, was behind the idea to paint the window surrounds white on the depot's Deltics whilst Allan, besides implementing this popular idea, is widely appreciated for his enthusiasm for the class and the many times that his Deltics were immaculately cleaned for special trains during his eight years at this depot. Allan is now Depot Manager at Eastleigh and Stuart is Traction Maintenance Engineer at Gateshead. *(Murray Brown)*

From 1 June a new through service from Edinburgh to Carlisle via Newcastle appeared in the timetable, the 0718 from Edinburgh and the 1553 return from Carlisle. Although rostered for class 47 haulage, the reduction in Deltic diagrams brought about by the introduction of more HST workings ensured that class 55 locomotives were regular performers on this train. On 7 September 1981 class 55 No 55019 *Royal Highland Fusilier* had a day out to Carlisle and was photographed on its return journey at Hexham. *(John Chalcraft)*

The Eastern Region ran an unprecedented series of Deltic specials to mark the passing of this famous class. One of these was from Finsbury Park to Bournemouth on 17 October 1981. No 55015 *Tulyar* with white window surrounds painted for the occasion by Finsbury Park depot is pictured here at Bournemouth. York depot later painted out the window surrounds when the complete locomotive was repainted! *(John Chalcraft)*

7

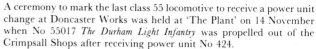

A ceremony to mark the last class 55 locomotive to receive a power unit change at Doncaster Works was held at 'The Plant' on 14 November when No 55017 *The Durham Light Infantry* was propelled out of the Crimpsall Shops after receiving power unit No 424.

Works Manager Ian McDonald presented a special chrome plated driver's key to David Russell, Traction Engineer, CM & EE Department, York, who then 'launched' the Deltic on its last few weeks in service by cracking a bottle of champagne on the buffer. *(Gerald Green)*

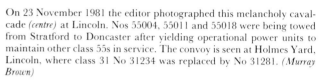

On 23 November 1981 the editor photographed this melancholy cavalcade *(centre)* at Lincoln. Nos 55004, 55011 and 55018 were being towed from Stratford to Doncaster after yielding operational power units to maintain other class 55s in service. The convoy is seen at Holmes Yard, Lincoln, where class 31 No 31234 was replaced by No 31281. *(Murray Brown)*

The use of Deltics on scheduled services ended on 31 December. On that date No 55017 *The Durham Light Infantry* was rostered to power the 1603 Kings Cross-York, the last Deltic-hauled service train to depart the London terminus.

Unofficially titled 'The Deltic City Tribute' and bearing a second headboard proclaiming 20 years service on the East Coast Main Line, No 55017 was photographed storming through Wood Green. However, enthusiasts awaiting the train's arrival at York suffered a bitter disappointment when the 1603 was delayed by a broken rail at Barkston and subsequently was terminated at Grantham. Here the Deltic was run round its train to form a scratch semi-fast back to Kings Cross. During the course of this journey No 55017 failed at Knebworth and suffered the indignity of being towed into Kings Cross by a class 47. Thus *The Durham Light Infantry* earned the unexpected accolade of being the last Deltic both to leave and arrive at Kings Cross in 'ordinary' service. For those sufficiently patient to wait at York, the two headboards in the picture arrived from the north on the nose of No 55019 *Royal Highland Fusilier* heading the 1630 Aberdeen-York, thanks to the efforts of enthusiasts who made their way from Grantham to Darlington to ensure that this very final Deltic-hauled service train reached its destination in style. *(Brian Cooke)*

With the closure of Finsbury Park depot for maintenance purposes and the transfer of the depot's surviving Deltics to York, the decision was taken to remove the Park's trademark—the white window surrounds applied to give an identity and to boost staff morale during a difficult period. With the exception of 55012 *Crepello,* which went to Doncaster Works for scrapping still sporting white surrounds, all Finsbury Park's class 55s reverted to blue surrounds shortly before their transfer to York. No 55009 *Alycidon,* however, remained in white in order to work the 'Finsbury Park Farewell' on 31 May 1981. It was painted blue the next day. Memories of this very popular adornment are recalled with this view of 55015 *Tulyar* reposing in the afternoon sunlight in, of all places, Harrogate goods yard where it was stabled with the empty stock of a 'Merrymaker' special from Kings Cross on 16 May. *(Murray Brown)*

The passing of the Deltics is epitomised in this late afternoon sunset panorama showing a Deltic on the principal service on which the class ended—the York semi-fasts. No 55013 *The Black Watch* nears journey's end at York with the 1403 from Kings Cross on 7 October 1981. *(Peter Skelton)*

The date of 2 August witnessed two very surprising outings for class 55s over routes on which hitherto these locomotives had not been seen. The Scottish Region ran a tour from Edinburgh to Oban and the Eastern Region ran an excursion from Newcastle to Whitby. Both tours were so successful that repeat runs were organised, the Oban tour taking place on 23 August and the Whitby trip running on 31 August. No 55021 *Argyle & Sutherland Highlander* officiated on both Oban trains whilst No 55002 *Kings Own Yorkshire Light Infantry* worked both Whitby trains. The return Oban special is pictured at Taynuilt on 23 August and No 55002 (left) is seen threading its way out of Whitby on 31 August. *(Colin Boocock, Murray Brown)*

On 5 November 1981 at York was staged a remarkable treat for Deltic afficionados, a line-up of the four class 55s which had been specially cleaned or repainted to work the Deltic farewell tours, Nos 55002, 55009, 55015 and 55022. The line-up, staged for official photographic purposes, was conditional on the weather—in the event, blue sky and sunshine! No 55022 *Royal Scots Grey* had failed the previous day whilst being trialled on a Liverpool turn and required a replacement power unit. To this end No 55011, which was at that time running on one power unit only, was authorised for withdrawal so that the operational power unit could be installed in No 55022 to render it capable of taking its place in the pool of 'special' class 55s. *(Murray Brown)*

APT in the news

Technical difficulties unfortunately delayed the APT from commencing revenue earning service until December but exhaustive testing and modifications took place during the year. Here one of the APT-P sets is undergoing tilt trials at Lamington in July 1981. *(Colin Boocock)*

The public had the opportunity of seeing at close hand this fine train when six APT-P vehicles were exhibited at Crewe Works Open Day on 5 June 1981. *(Barry Nicolle)*

In the weeks leading up to the public launching of APT services on 7 December, assessment and staff familiarisation runs were conducted between Glasgow and London. Here unit No 370 006 leans into the curve at Winwick Junction during a southbound run on 23 November. (D Lowe)

The first week of public service for APT-P was one of mixed fortunes but on the inaugural southbound run on 7 December unit No 370 002 behaved impeccably, accomplishing the 401¼ mile journey from Glasgow Central to Euston in four hours 14 minutes 50 seconds—an average speed of over 94 mph, with a maximum of 137mph. At the end of this historic run, the first revenue earning APT arrives at Euston, where BRB Chairman Sir Peter Parker greeted the crew, co-drivers Frank Addis and Joe Baker. Technical difficulties during subsequent runs with the train led BR to withdraw it from public service pending further tests. (Both: *Brian Cooke*)

July saw the unit in the West Country. On the first of that month, the prototype approaches Bristol Temple Meads prior to its press run to Weston-Super-Mare. *(John Chalcraft)*

Class 140 on trial

In 1981 BR proudly unveiled its low cost class 140 two-car lightweight dmu. Based on the Lightweight Experimental Vehicle (LEV) produced in 1978 by BR in collaboration with Leyland Vehicles Ltd, the class 140 weighs 38 tons and seats 102 passengers, with additional standing room. The body, which employs bus construction techniques, was supplied by Leyland's Workington factory. BR fabricated the underframe and final assembly took place at BREL Derby Litchurch Lane. Top speed is 75 mph.

After initial trials the unit embarked on a nationwide tour, giving demonstration runs for the benefit of local councils and PTEs. Leeds was the first of these venues, and it was to this city that the class 140 returned in October to begin regular service evaluation on the Leeds-Barnsley-Sheffield service.

The accompanying pictures show a few of the many places visited by this potentially important new train during the course of the year.

The class 140 leaves Bradford Exchange to return to Leeds in June. *(BR Eastern Region)*

The venue for the unit on 22 June 1981 was Newcastle Central where it was on view before trials on the Newcastle-Carlisle line. *(Barry Nicolle)*

After a spell on the WR the unit returned to the ER and was photographed at Cambridge on 8 July 1981. *(Keith Grafton)*

Shortly afterwards the destination was Scotland, where three weeks of trials were undertaken in the Strathclyde PTE area. In this view, the train awaits departure with the 1605 Cumbernauld-Springburn on 12 August 1981. Note that the leading vehicle, No 55501, now has sliding toplights on all windows. *(Colin Boocock)*

On 14 September 1981 a three-week period of service commenced on the Colne-Preston run. This picture shows the 1346 train from Colne approaching Nelson. Both vehicles are now modified with sliding toplights. *(Tom Heavyside)*

Driving Trailer Open Second (DTOS), with a seating capacity of 74. *(Keith Grafton)*

MSE stock appears

A fleet of 48 4-car thyristor controlled class 317 emus has been ordered from BREL for the Midland Suburban Electrification. Vehicle design is based on that of the Mk III coach and the units depart in concept from the earlier class 313 and its derivatives in the adoption of all steel rather than aluminium body construction and the abandonment of the principle of 50% of axles motored in favour of only four per unit. Top speed is 145 km/h (90 mph).

The trailer cars are constructed at BREL Derby Litchurch Lane then railed to York, where the power cars are built, to be formed into complete units prior to despatch to the St Pancras-Bedford line.

Power Motor Open Second (PMOS). This vehicle, which seats 79, carries the pantograph and all traction equipment. Combined output of the four traction motors is 760kW (1020hp). Bogies are of the new BP20 type. *(Keith Grafton)*

Interior view of a DTOS vehicle. Note the metal hopper ventilators above the windows. *(BR LMR)*

Nearing completion at Derby in August was DTOS No 54001 while the unit's power car is just visible to the right.

In the works yard TOS No 57000 was exhibited. *(both: Keith Grafton)*

Class 210 demu shown at Derby

Visitors to BREL Derby Litchurch Lane Open Day on 8 August were able to inspect at close quarters equipment for the second class 210 demu prototype, No 210 002. This is a 3-car unit powered by a floor-mounted 915kW (1225hp) German MTU 12-cylinder "vee" engine with GEC ac/dc transmission. Four-car sister unit 210 001 has a 6-cylinder GEC engine derived from that of the HST with Brush traction equipment.

No 210 002 is second class only with seating for 203 passengers. Formation is Driving Motor Brake Open Second (DMBOS) containing all power and transmission equipment, Trailer Open Second (TOS) and Driving Trailer Open Second (DTOS). The two units share many common features with the MSE class 317 emus (opposite), including bogie, traction motor and general vehicle design, and can operate in multiple with these and future similar emu types. Both units were expected to be handed over for service evaluation in 1982.

With the winter timetable change on 5 January 1981 both Middlesbrough and Hull became new destinations for HST services. In this view taken at Eaglescliffe on 19 May 1981, the down 'Cleveland Executive' is approaching from the south. To the right are the lines to Darlington. *(Tom Heavyside)*

HST developments

BR ran a special HST on 1 March to mark the 125th anniversary of the London, Tilbury & Southend Railway. A headboard was carried and the train is seen pulling into Liverpool Street, the first HST to do so, on arrival from Southend. The special was permitted to run up to 100mph between Upminster and Barking. *(Keith Grafton)*

A timing trial using a HST set took place in the early hours of 20 March 1981 from Sheffield to St Pancras and return. This proving run was made at the request of Sheffield City authorities and several councillors accompanied the train. Neville Hill depot, Leeds, provided the set which worked empty to Sheffield Midland and thence to St Pancras, departing at 0040. Normal line speeds were not exceeded and a return to Sheffield was made at 0405. In the event a HST service was not established but BR, conscious of the need for further improvements to the Midland route, later confirmed the transfer of four HST sets from the WR to the Midland line commencing with the 1982 October timetable change. The special HST is pictured at St Pancras after arriving at 0305 on 20 March. Power car No 43108 leads the train. *(Keith Grafton)*

The start of the summer timetable witnessed the first through HST from Glasgow to Kings Cross. The HST, the 0945 SuO from Queen Street, with power car 43084 leading (43089 at the rear) is seen forging up Cowlairs incline on 7 June 1981, the inaugural day of operation. *(Colin Boocock)*

HST units began to operate certain North-East/South-West services from 5 October, so ending the recent comparative supremacy on this artery of class 45, 46 and 47 locomotives. Here power car No 43171 heads the 0700 Bristol-Leeds at Sheffield Midland on 26 October 1981. On the left, class 45 No 45117 has arrived with the 0750 from St Pancras. *(Keith Grafton)*

The 0820 Plymouth-Leeds HST with power car No 43171 again in the viewfinder accelerates away from Gloucester with the cathedral piercing the skyline. The date was 27 October 1981.
(Peter Skelton)

The WR's Mk 3 'generator set' was disbanded from 12 October 1981. The train had been formed of HST trailer vehicles made available when power car traction motor problems, since resolved, delayed full introduction of the WR's second batch of HSTs, Nos 253 028-253 041. To provide power for on train services such as heating and air conditioning, the WR acquired the CM & EE Department's generator van No ADB 975325, which entered traffic on 1 September 1980.

On 30 August 1981, the set is seen heading west out of Bristol through Parson Street with an excursion. The generator van is immediately behind the locomotive, No 47289.
(John Chalcraft)

20

American in Britain

In January 1981, Somerset quarrying company Foster Yeoman took delivery from General Motors of this locomotive to shunt its Torr Works facility at Merehead, near Shepton Mallet. Built at GM's La Grange, Illinois, plant, the machine is of this manufacturer's standard SW1001 type and is powered by an eight-cylinder two-stroke engine developing 1100hp gross. Transmission is electric. Although GM locomotives are plentiful in Ireland, this example is believed to be the only one in service on the British mainland. Foster Yeoman has numbered its acquisition 44 and bestowed on it the name *Western Yeoman 11* with nameplates finished in correct class 52 style! In this view, No 44 is seen on 8 July propelling loaded tipplers through the water sprinkler (to reduce dust nuisance) and into the exchange sidings at Merehead. In the background, Nos 37297 and 37224 await release after arrival with empty hoppers. *(Ken Harris)*

All dressed up

Unofficial (and official) livery variations continue to delight the enthusiast. No 08889, photographed at Coldham Lane carriage sidings, Cambridge, on 13 October, is obviously the pride of Cambridge depot, with red bufferbeams and running plates and, in best Stratford tradition, a white roof. *(Barry Nicolle)*

End of C & D

The cessation in 1981 of BR's C & D business brought to an end traffic from the Brian Mills depot in Sunderland. At one time, three trains left this depot daily but this was eroded to one in the final months. No 45011 brings in the Bristol-Sunderland BMD parcels on 27 March and is pictured at Wearmouth Junction, Sunderland. *(Peter Robinson)*

When this picture was taken on 5 September 1981 it gave a foresight of the future motive power scene on the Blyth & Tyne line, for shortly afterwards Gateshead depot received an allocation of class 56 locomotives for intended use on the Blyth power station traffic. No 56093 was photographed at Blyth Cambois working from Butterwell open cast site to Blyth power station. *(Peter Robinson)*

56s break new ground

Early in the year, a number of class 56 locomotives were loaned to the Stoke Division for crew training, although the stay was brief due to 'operating difficulties'. In this view (centre left) of Cockshute shed, Stoke, Nos 56070, 56065 and 56054 await duty on 14 February 1981. (Barry Nicolle)

Deliveries of new class 56 locomotives from Doncaster Works continued throughout 1981. A spotless 56094 destined for Tinsley depot waits to leave 'The Plant' on 26 July 1981. Units handed over for traffic during the year were Nos 56090-56103. (John Chalcraft)

One of the Stoke duties for the visiting class 56 locomotives was the 1126SX Trentham Sidings-Fiddlers Ferry power station mgr service. No 56054 (below) motors through Barthomley with this train on 13 February 1981. (Barry Nicolle)

Another area into which class 56 locomotives were drafted for crew training preparatory to official allocation was the north-east. Thornaby and Gateshead depots were host to this class. No 56083, the last class 56 to be out-shopped in the old livery, heads a southbound chemical train near Stockton on 19 May 1981. (Tom Heavyside)

The closure of the MSW electrified route brought to an end the careers of the remaining class 76 locomotives. The survivors at the cessation of the service were worked back to the LMR and congregated at Guide Bridge and Reddish depot. Reddish blues are evident in this sad picture of locomotives 76015, 76040, 76037, 76049, 76004, 76055 and 76052 awaiting disposal on 13 September 1981. *(Tom Heavyside)*

Retirements

Last year saw the demise of several locomotive classes while other types had numerous members condemned.

The last of the class 31/0 "Toffee-apples", No 31019, was withdrawn early in the year. It was purposely not robbed of parts to enable it to be offered for sale. However, despite more than one offer from preservationists, BR considered that the bids were too low and did not match the value of the main spares. Accordingly, No 31019 was despatched to Swindon for cutting up. Luckily, the "Toffee-apple" locomotive, so named after the driver's control handle in the cab, is represented for future generations by No D5500 (ex No 31018) at the NRM, York. No 31019 was photographed at Stratford on 8 April just before consignment to Swindon. *(Ken Harris)*

The first of the strange looking but very functional class 13 locomotives was condemned at Tinsley on 28 June 1981. No 13002 was converted to its present form in 1965 from two separate shunters, Nos D3697 and D4187. A defect on the cabless unit, the 'slave', precipitated withdrawal but No 13002 was later despatched to Swindon Works to establish if the 'master' unit could be converted to an air-braked shunter. No 13002 is pictured at Tinsley on 13 August before removal to Swindon. *(Murray Brown)*

The long reign of the diminutive class 06 shunters came to an end in 1981. Dundee was the final home of the class with No 06002, withdrawn 7 September, being the last to survive in stock. No 06003 has been given a reprieve in Departmental service based at Reading (see p 52). No 06002 also made the journey south to Reading. The picture shows No 06005 stored at Dundee in April 1981 together with sister locomotive No 06006. *(Colin Boocock)*

Swindon Works yard in 1981 continued to receive numerous locomotives of various classes mothballed or withdrawn either because of planned withdrawal or the recession. Just like Barry scrapyard, however, locomotives are extracted from time to time. Class 20 No 20050, formerly No D8000, was assured of posterity when it left in October to become the property of the NRM, but other locomotives temporarily reprieved will no doubt one day return to Swindon for good! Class 46 No 46054 was heading the line of stored locomotives on 12 February in the company of Nos 46022, 46021, 46010, 25040 and 45021. *(Keith Grafton)*

The Mk 3 sleeping car made its long awaited debut in 1981. There are two types of vehicle, the SLEP (either class with pantry) and the SLE (either class). The latter has 13 sleeping compartments whilst the SLEP has 12 plus an attendant's compartment. Controlled emission toilets are standard equipment and the vehicles run on BT10 bogies.

In all, 120 SLEP and 90 SLE cars have been ordered from BREL, the first 95 being destined for the ER. First examples were delivered in November and after commissioning at York proving/delivery runs were made to Bounds Green depot, London. Craigentinny (Edinburgh) and Aberdeen depots were also allocated vehicles for staff familiarisation. The formal handing over of the new vehicles took place on 10 December at Derby Litchurch Lane Works when BRB Chief Passenger Manager Peter Keen was handed a ceremonial key to SLEP No E10514 and SLE No E10655 by Michael Casey, Engineering Director of BREL. A press demonstration run was made on 18 December from Edinburgh to Kings Cross and first scheduled ECML services using the new stock were due to begin on 11 January 1982. It was announced by BR that journeys using the vehicles would attract a supplementary charge. Already in 1981, as a prelude to introduction of these new vehicles to revenue service, inroads were being made into the stock of Mk 1 sleepers.

Here SLE No E10649 is seen on view at the Open Day at BREL's Derby Litchurch Lane Works on 8 August. The vehicle is air-braked only and features built-in electric tail lamps. *(Keith Grafton)*

Mk 3 sleepers are delivered

The comfortable appointments of the Mk 3 sleeper appear even more welcoming in this wintry study of a rake of the new vehicles taken at Doncaster in the small hours of 15 December during a commissioning run from Kings Cross to Edinburgh. *(Gary Grafton)*

Prior to delivery to the ER for acceptance, new sleeping cars were trialled up the Midland main line from Derby and were also subject to more detailed testing as seen in this view taken at Crewe on 27 August 1981 of class 86 No 86253 *The Manchester Guardian* hauling a Carnforth-Wolverhampton sleeper test train and utilising one of the CM & EE Department's Test Coaches. *(Barry Nicolle)*

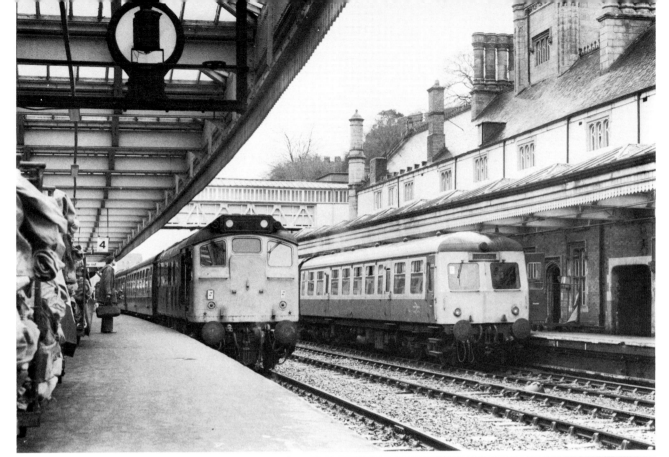

Commencement of the summer timetable on 1 June 1981 saw the introduction of class 33 locomotives on the Crewe-Cardiff service, quite an event in the eyes of the enthusiast fraternity. The old order is illustrated in this view at Shrewsbury on 7 March of class 25 No 25060 at the head of the 1024 Cardiff-Crewe. A Chester-bound Swindon-built dmu, a reminder of an earlier era on the Cardiff-Crewe line, waits at the little used No 3 platform. *(Ken Harris)*

In connection with this changeover, an extensive crew training programme was implemented and over 30 different class 33 locomotives were recorded on training runs. A very unusual sight at Crewe is No 33025 crossing North Junction with stock for the 1400 driver training special to Shrewsbury Crewe Bank on 6 May 1981. Usually when the service ran, it arrived and departed from the south end of the station and the locomotive ran round on No 1 through road. *(Barry Nicolle)*

33s take over Cardiff-Crewe

Ironically on the first day of the new timetable the only Crewe-Cardiff service to be class 33 hauled was the 1602 from Crewe. Here it is seen with No 33022 idling at the helm before departure. *(Barry Nicolle)*

All was dark at Burnley Station on Friday 13 March when suddenly the lights went on and class 86/2 electric No 86213 was in the spotlight, ready to be named *Lancashire Witch*. Official dignitaries included the Mayor and Mayoress of Pendle and the Mayor and Mayoress of Burnley. (*BR LMR, Preston*)

The name game

BR continued its much applauded policy of naming locomotives during 1981, achieving considerable valuable publicity as a result. Besides further class 47 and 86 locomotives being so decorated, the Western Region decided to commemorate and identify its achievements by naming some class 56 freight locomotives. Locomotives named during the year were:-

JANUARY
86103 André Chapelon
86257 Snowdon

FEBRUARY
86260 Driver Wallace Oakes G.C.
86261 Driver John Axon G.C.

MARCH
86207 City of Lichfield
86213 Lancashire Witch
86227 Sir Henry Johnson
86248 Sir Clwyd/County of Clwyd

APRIL
47711 Greyfriars Bobby
47712 Lady Diana Spencer
86215 Joseph Chamberlain

MAY
37180 Sir Dyfed/County of Dyfed
47444 University of Nottingham
86102 Robert A. Riddles

JUNE
56038 Western Mail
86230 The Duke of Wellington

JULY
47158 Henry Ford
56037 Richard Trevithick

AUGUST
33025 Sultan
37026 Loch Awe
37027 Loch Eil
37043 Loch Lomond
37081 Loch Long

SEPTEMBER
47577 James Nightall G.C.
47579 Benjamin Gimbert G.C.
86249 County of Merseyside

OCTOBER
86247 Abraham Darby

NOVEMBER
47402 Gateshead
56035 Taff Merthyr
86242 James Kennedy G.C.
86244 The Royal British Legion
86256 Pebble Mill

DECEMBER
47401 North Eastern
47406 Rail-Riders

On 30 April 1981 Mr Robert Cooney flags off the 0930 Glasgow-Edinburgh hauled by No 47712 *Lady Diana Spencer* watched by Leslie J Soane, General Manager, ScR, and Sir Peter Parker, Chairman, BRB. Sir Peter had formally named the locomotive at an earlier ceremony. Although invited to the ceremony, Lady Diana had been unable to attend but sent a telegram to the General Manager thanking him and expressing her best wishes to all those connected with the ceremony and the future running of the locomotive. Mr Robert Cooney was the winner of a competition staged by Radio Clyde to find a suitable name. Sir Peter later travelled to Edinburgh to name officially No 47711 *Greyfriars Bobby*. This name was the winning entry in a competition staged by Radio Forth and recalls the little Edinburgh mongrel which maintained a poignant 14-year vigil beside its master's grave in Greyfriars cemetery. *(BR ScR)*

On 28 May 1981, Mr Tom George, immediate past Chairman of Dyfed County Council named class 37 No 37180 *Sir Dyfed/County of Dyfed* at Carmarthen station. This bi-lingual name marks the practical support and interest shown by Dyfed County Council in rail transport matters, notably its contribution to the cost of improvements at Llanelli and Pembroke Dock stations. *(Keith Grafton)*

Following the ceremony, No 37180 was assigned to work the 1115 Swansea-Milford Haven train which it worked forward from Carmarthen. *(BR WR-Cardiff)*

Both the London Midland and Eastern Regions commemorated brave drivers in 1981, the first ceremony taking place at Euston on 19 February 1981 when Driver John Axon G.C. and Driver Wallace Oakes G.C. had their names unveiled on two class 86 locomotives. Here Mrs Axon officiates at the ceremony in recognition of the bravery of her late husband when in 1957 he succeeded in stopping his defective train despite sustaining fatal injuries. *(BR LMR)*

Mr Duncan Gardiner had an enjoyable day on 2 June 1981 when in his capacity as Editor of the locally based 'Western Mail' newspaper, he unveiled an appropriate nameplate on No 56038, the first class 56 to be named. On the left of the photograph is Mr Albert Barnes, South Wales Divisional Manager. *(Keith Grafton)*

Following its naming, No 56038 gave photographers a rare treat by working the 1210 Cardiff-Portsmouth as far as Bristol. In sparkling condition, the locomotive is seen here starting its train out of Newport. *(H J Ashman)*

A day out with a difference for a class 56 locomotive took place on 23 July when No 56037 set off from Cardiff hauling a replica of Richard Trevithick's "Penydarren Locomotive". The 56 was later named *Richard Trevithick* by Mrs Cherry Mitchell, great great great grand-daughter of the Cornish engineer, at a ceremony at Merthyr. On the train's return to Cardiff, a 15-minute stop was made at Abercynon, terminus of the Merthyr tramroad on which ran the original Penydarren locomotive in 1804. *(both: BR WR-Cardiff)*

Dual naming ceremonies took place at March station on 28 September 1981 when nameplates were unveiled on two class 47 locomotives in memory of enginemen James Nightall G.C. and Benjamin Gimbert G.C. whose heroic efforts with a blazing ammunition train saved the town of Soham, Cambridgeshire in the early hours of 2 June 1944. No 47577 was named *Benjamin Gimbert G.C.* by Mrs Violet Gimbert and No 47579 *James Nightall G.C.* by Mr Baker representing the Nightall family. Mrs Gimbert is pictured standing next to Mr Clement Freud MP for Isle of Ely, and Mr Baker. (Both: *Keith Grafton*)

37s take the high road

At the commencement of the summer timetable class 37 locomotives took over most West Highland line duties. Displaced class 37s, mostly from East Anglia, had been moving into Scotland for several months and the final certification that they were in Scotland to stay came with the naming of four members of the class after Scottish lochs. No 37025 stands at Oban at the head of the 1226 to Glasgow Queen Street alongside class 27 No 27205 shunting a local freight on 22 June 1981. (*John Chalcraft*)

Just another class 37 undergoing classified repair? Well not quite, for No 37292 is the first of three class 37 locomotives to be uprated to 2,000hp for use in Scotland. The locomotive was pictured in Doncaster Works on 31 July 1981. (*Barry Nicolle*)

The changing scene is not just confined to passenger workings. No 37037 leaves Crainlarich with the daily Glasgow Sighthill-Corpach air-braked freight on 22 June 1981. (*John Chalcraft*)

1981 was to have been the last year for the class 46 locomotives but a change of decision in the autumn resulted in a temporary reprieve. Numerous withdrawn members of the class had been sent to Swindon Works and BREL had received an enquiry from abroad to purchase a batch, but in the event the sale was not concluded. Some illustration of the far ranging and varied duties of this class may be gained from these 1981 views of No 46044 easing into Gloucester station with the 1432 Paignton-York on 29 July and sister locomotive 46046 on more menial duties near Morpeth on 22 June while working a DCE trip from Belford to Tyne Yard. (Both: *Barry Nicolle*)

Class 46 swan song

The first class 47 locomotive painted by BREL Crewe in the new style livery was No 47711. The second 47/7 in such colours, No 47712, later to be named *Lady Diana Spencer* poses behind Crewe depot on its way to the holding sidings on 14 April. This locomotive was also the last of the current batch of class 47/7 conversions. *(Barry Nicolle)*

A new look came to some Scottish Region class 47 locomotives with the addition of miniature snowploughs. Inverness-based class 47/4 No 47550 was on exhibition at the Crewe Works Open Day having been fitted with snowploughs whilst undergoing light overhaul. Note how the eth jumper cables have to be resited for this modification. *(Barry Nicolle)*

47s in the news

No-one really expected Stratford depot not to stage some spectacular for the national event of the year and so it was that class 47/4 No 47583 *County of Hertfordshire* was proudly unveiled by Stratford at its Open Day on 11 July 1981. At this time, the large double-arrow was plain white with the blue and red embellishments being added later for the Wedding Day. In this latter guise No 47583 is waiting at Liverpool Street on 13 August with the 1230 to Norwich. The extended white bands were painted out in mid-December. *(Keith Grafton)*

All change on the GE

The new order for the GE, thyristor controlled class 315 units 845, 846 and 851, wait to begin their careers at Stratford on 15 April 1981. Deliveries of this type were completed during 1981. *(Barry Nicolle)*

Two views showing class 315 in service depict Nos 315 819 and 315 833 leaving Stratford with the 1358 Liverpool Street-Gidea Park on 8 April and No 315 810 arriving at Liverpool Street forming the 1156 from Gidea Park on 15 September. *(Ken Harris, Keith Grafton)*

From 20 July 1981, the Clacton branch became host to class 313 units seconded from recast Great Northern services. Passing Romford on 17 July 1981 in readiness for their new role are units 313 008, 313 037 and 313 035, forming a rare 9-car formation of this type. *(Keith Grafton)*

The date of 3 October 1981 witnessed the end of 32 years of class 306 service on the Liverpool Street-Gidea Park-Shenfield run. On this day a farewell railtour was organised by the RCTS, the train being formed of 3 class 306 units, numbers 017/084/037. Unit 037 was the last to receive an overhaul at Wolverton Works in February 1981.

The tour departed from Liverpool Street for Shoeburyness via Upminster-Ockendon branch-Grays-Tilbury Angle West-East Jct-Pitsea. The train then continued to Southend Central, a place that class 306 units visited occasionally, such as on Bank Holidays to act as 'hooligan specials' for bringing revellers and troublemakers back to London from Southend. The tour continued to Fenchurch Street via Barking then on to Colchester, travelling via the little used Gas Factory Jct-Bow Jct-Stratford route and the main line to Colchester. Returning to Shenfield, the last 306 special journeyed to Southend Victoria and finally back to Liverpool Street.

See p 87 for an ironic tailpiece to the class 306 story.

Two class 306 units led by No 007 prepare to depart for Gidea Park with the 1438 train on 16 April 1981. *(Ken Harris)*

Apart from a small number of vehicles withdrawn following fire or collision damage, the first 70 vehicles of class 306 were condemned on 10 March and stabled at Stanway awaiting disposal. The majority of remaining vehicles were condemned in large batches and moved to Whitemoor Down Storage yard and March station. Pictured at the latter location on 19 July 1981 were two lines of units headed by 070 and 078. *(Ken Harris)*

Driver Colin Rhodes of Stratford poses in front of unit 017 at Shoeburyness, a place previously not visited by this class, before the train continued to Fenchurch Street. *(Keith Grafton)*

The final day of class 306 service and a chance of a rare picture. The RCTS special stands in Liverpool Street with Shoeburyness as its destination. Unit 037 leads train. *(Keith Grafton)*

Refurbishment of emu stock is taking place on the Eastern Region where class 302, 307 and 309 units are receiving major attention. The first of the 32 class 307 'Southend converted' unit (so named because this class was originally delivered for dc operation and was later converted to ac) was exhibited at Liverpool Street station on 15 September 1981. This view of set 120, the first renovated under a £21m programme, shows vehicle E75120 sporting a headboard appropriate for the occasion proclaiming 'Restyled Commuter Train' and referring to the 7-year programme to refurbish 820 vehicles. This vehicle is now a DTC (Driving Trailer Composite) having formerly been a DTSO (Driving Trailer Second Open). As its new designation states, a first class section is now included. One door has been removed in this section. *(Keith Grafton)*

An important innovation in the refurbishment of the class 307 units is the provision of gangway connections, illustrated in this picture between MS E61020 and TC (Trailer Composite) E70020. The young lady standing on top of the Motor Second appears to have a solution to overcrowding that would not gain BR approval. *(Keith Grafton)*

A general view of No 307 120 at Liverpool Street on 15 September 1981. Front end modifications include removal of the redundant route indicator panel from between the windows and the provision of marker lights above each buffer. *(Keith Grafton)*

The new look of MS (Motor Second) E61020 in set 120. Note the 2 + 3 seating arrangement, tartan seat covers, 2-tier luggage and coat racks, fluorescent lighting and end doors providing access to all coaches within the unit. *(Keith Grafton)*

Class 302 emus from the Great Eastern section are now overhauled at Eastleigh, presenting a new view to photographers on the South Western main line. Returning from Eastleigh in pristine condition are sets Nos 219 and 241 hauled by class 33/1 No 33104. These trains are routed up the LSWR main line and thence via Kensington Olympia, Willesden High Level Junction, Dalston West Junction, Channelsea Junction and Stratford to Ilford. On the day this picture was taken, 13 November 1981, the locomotive and train had come to the assistance of the 0940 Poole-Manchester hauled by class 47/4 No 47432 which had expired en route. The cavalcade is seen at Basingstoke. *(Keith Grafton)*

This interior view of unit No 302 304 (a Motor Brake Second) 'opened out' by the removal of compartment partitions makes an interesting comparison to that of MS E61020 in set 307 120 on the previous page. The original lights and ventilators have been retained. *(Keith Grafton)*

Live on the Midland

Energising the Bedford-Luton Hoo section of the MSE scheme in January 1981 enabled the LMR to embark in March on a programme of staff instruction using class 315 emus borrowed from the ER. The first unit concerned, No 315 807, is pictured here at Luton preparing to return to Bedford during a crew training run on 15 May. *(Ken Harris)*

A surprise was waiting in 1981 for observers who thought the end of the line had been reached with milk traffic, for a new fleet of tankers took to the rails in the late summer and autumn. The wagons were built by W H Davis Ltd and utilised old underframes from former BR tankers with new tanks. The fleet consisted of three batches, 40 2-axle wagons numbered 42800-42839, 26 3-axle wagons numbered 42840-42865 with a further batch of 5 numbered 42866-42870. A rake of these tankers is pictured at Chard in August 1981. The first duty on which they were engaged was a daily working to Stowmarket. *(Ken Groom)*

Home with the milk—again

The BRE-Leyland railbus, known as R3 when delivered but later numbered in the Research Department fleet as RDB 977020, made its colourful debut in 1981. Prior to entry into revenue earning service on the Bristol-Severn Beach line in October, the railbus was thoroughly tested on BR's Old Dalby test track, at which location it was photographed on 19 June. *(Basil Hancock)*

Railbuses new and old

The railbus wheel has turned full circle in 20 years and two survivors from the first generation of railbuses active on the Keighley and Worth Valley Railway were sparkling in their former liveries following repainting. One of these, No E79962 enhances the rural scene at Oxenhope on 15 August and is sporting the original yellow 'whiskers'. *(Basil Hancock)*

The Scottish Region, besides holding the distinction of being the first region to complete its emu fleet in blue and grey livery, also achieved the same with its dmu fleet. However, it should be pointed out that some regions are only using the blue and grey livery on refurbished units. This photograph shows class 116 set No 160 approaching Glasgow Central on a working from Edinburgh Waverley via Shotts on 21 March 1981. The Trans-Clyde motif can be seen, denoting the link with the Strathclyde PTE. *(Colin Boocock)*

Dmu modifications

1981 saw completion of the fitting of sealed steel plates in place of gangways on the former intermediate power cars of ScR class 126. This innovation was intended to reduce draughts and improve the driver's environment. The work is evident in this picture of the rear of an Ayr-Glasgow train leaving Paisley. *(Colin Boocock)*

In 1981 the decision was taken to remove the power units from the intermediate power cars of the 'Trans-Pennine' dmu sets to reduce operating costs. The reduction in journey time across the Pennines with 800 rather than 1200hp was negligible and the modification was implemented on ten vehicles, thus converting them to trailer cars. Various circuitry and physical alterations were also required, the major work being the provision of an alternative source of power to charge the batteries. This was accomplished by fitting a pulley to the final drive which in turn drives an alternator to supply the battery feed. The last of the ten vehicles to be modified had its last run in original condition on 29 October. On completion all ten vehicles were renumbered in the series E59833-42. A rather bare looking trailer car, formerly No E51974 and now renumbered No E59835, waits at Sheffield Midland on 31 July 1981. *(Barry Nicolle)*

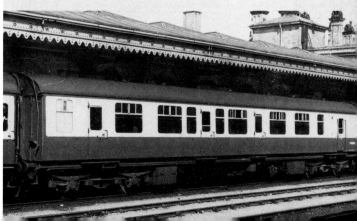

Locomotive-hauled
vice dmu . . .

The North Wales run became a paradise for class 40 devotees and BR made considerable (and unpredicted?) revenue from admirers of this class. Here No 40121 moves a Manchester Victoria-Bangor train out of Llandudno Junction on 11 July 1981. *(Les Nixon)*

The LMR offered passengers vastly improved conditions from introduction of the summer timetable when the Manchester-North Wales service was rostered for locomotive hauled Mk 1 stock. This route was one of several on which BR was planning to utilise locomotives and coaches in place of dmu operation and this process will be continuing in 1982.

Class 47/4 No 47537 leaves Warrington with the 1338 Bangor-Manchester Victoria on 10 October 1981. *(Tom Heavyside)*

From 5 October the Scottish Region recast Edinburgh-Dundee local service with class 26 haulage and a light load of Mk 1 stock, usually in the order of four coaches. Class 27 locomotives were also observed on this service but No 26012 was officiating on 10 October when photographed climbing to the Forth Bridge on a service from Dundee. *(Peter Robinson)*

. . . and push-pull to the Granite City

An interesting development on Glasgow-Aberdeen services commenced on 2 February 1981 when the 0740 and 1535 services from Glasgow (return services 1140 and 1950 from Aberdeen) were diagrammed for a push-pull set. The train consists of a standard Edinburgh-Glasgow Mk 3/2 push-pull set with an additional dual-braked RMB catering vehicle marshalled next to the locomotive. On 7 April 1981, No 47711 propels the 1140 out of Aberdeen and passes the small Clayhills carriage and HST inspection shed. The magnificent signal gantry had numbered days as a new power box scheme was to make redundant the semaphore signals during 1981. *(Colin Boocock)*

Aggregate traffic yields a sizeable income for BR. These wagons were all built by Procor and are in the liveries of Tilbury Roadstone, Amey Roadstone, Tarmac, Yeoman and Hall Aggregates.

'Railfreight 81'

Dubbed 'Railfreight 81', the 1981 Private Wagon Exhibition was held at the Olympia Motorail Terminal, Kensington, from 3-7 March, 1981. The exhibition was organised by the Private Wagon Federation which represents the owners and users of private wagons and the wagon manufacturing, hiring and repair industries in the country and was opened by then Transport Secretary the Rt Hon Norman Fowler MP. Some 35 organisations took part and the highlight of the show was the many wagons on view, including some being displayed for the first time. Private wagons in use on BR total approximately 20,000 and this figure is steadily rising. It represents about 13% of the rail freight vehicles in Britain. Some of the 60 wagons on display at the exhibition are shown below. (all photographs: *Ken Harris* on 5 March 1981)

A 51 tonne glw two-axle scrap wagon exhibited by The Standard Railway Wagon Company.

Procor-built two-axle tarpaulin-sided wagon in the livery of Campbell's Soups Ltd. Eight of these colourful vehicles have been built.

BR exhibited one of its type VIX two-axle ferry wagons.

Class 86/2 86260 *Driver Wallace Oakes G.C.* sets the scene at Kensington in the incongruous company of Pullman Car *Topaz* (on hire to Resco Railways Ltd from the NRM) and a WR lower quadrant signal.

Also built by Procor is the Procar 80, one of ten high capacity double-deck car carrying vehicles built for Renault. Similar vehicles are operated by Tolemans.

German-built 1-B-1 (or is it a 2-4-2T?) based on the Mercedes-Benz Unimog truck with retractable guide wheels for rail application. The vehicle can move 600 tonnes.

SR's extensive facelift programme on class 415 4-EPB units continued in 1981. Modifications being made include the conversion of compartment accommodation to open saloons, provision of strip lighting and, in some vehicles, the addition of SR system maps. Completed units are turned out in blue and grey livery and renumbered in the 54XX series. Unusually for SR non-corridor emus the numbers are displayed over both cab windows, as evidenced by this view of No 5402 running into East Croydon on 15 April 1981. This set was the first to be refurbished by BREL Eastleigh, set No 5401 being a prototype completed by the SR. Horwich Works is also participating in the refurbishment programme. *(Barry Nicolle)*

2-HAP units, now in blue and grey livery, are a common sight again on the SR's South Western Division. Here No 6006 leads a pair of class 421 units past Earlsfield towards Waterloo on 31 March 1981. The 2-HAP units were redesignated 2-SAP with the removal of first class accommodation and worked Windsor line services in recent years. The first class sections were later reinstated and the units reverted to the 2-HAP designation. This particular unit, numbered 5906 when it was a 2-SAP, was one of the first HAP units to receive blue and grey livery. *(Colin Boocock)*

SR emu developments

Class 411 4-CEP refurbishment continued at Swindon during 1981 and although initially restricted to boat train workings, these units have become available for general South Eastern Division services as more have been returned to traffic. In all 108 units are to be refurbished and BR considered it necessary to retain a numerical distinction between those units supplied under Phase I of the Kent Coast electrification and those of Phase II. As the various units entered works in relation to their planned overhaul dates, the system adopted was to renumber Phase I units (originally Nos 7105-7153) from 1506 upwards and the Phase II units (originally Nos 7154-7211) from 1608 downwards! Just to confuse the issue, some early refurbished units carry the full BR six-digit number but as the SR uses a four digit numbering scheme, only the last four numbers are recognised and this system has since been adopted. An example of six-digit numbering is shown in the picture of No 411605 (in effect 1605) heading the 1114 Victoria-Maidstone East at Bromley South on 3 August 1981. One of the Phase II units, No 1593 is pictured leading the 1000 Victoria-Folkstone Harbour through Shortlands on 5 August. (Both: *Brian Garvin*)

On test on BR . . .

'Hydra' is the name of a Research and Development Division test bed for a new hydraulic transmission system. Former Cravens single unit parcels car, No M55997 has become No RDB 975385. One of its bogies has been replaced by a powered B4 bogie fitted with four Volvo fixed displacement 150cc/rev hydraulic motors. The vehicle's Leyland 680 engine drives two Rexroth Hydromatic axial piston pumps each of which supplies fluid to two motors incorporated into the axlebox, driving the axle directly. RDB 975385 has now run over 3,000 miles at speeds up to 68mph. Several advantages have been highlighted over conventional dmu transmission. Besides cheaper installation costs, these include harnessing full engine power during acceleration, up to 35 per cent less unsprung weight (saving track wear and tear) and the system's potential use for braking to save on expensive conventional brake maintenance. 'Hydra' retains its standard bogie at the other end with engine and mechanical transmission for comparative testing. *(BR Research Division)*

A new look for the Snowdon Mountain Railway? No, but the train illustrated does have connections with that famous line. This strange looking locomotive is a National Coal Board success story. It is a 91hp machine manufactured by the Hunslet Engine Co. Its development followed an NCB requirement to overcome the limitations which precludes the use of locomotives underground on gradients steeper than 1 in 15. This rack locomotive uses existing track with the addition of a rack section on the steeper sections. It is a new design and includes a major transmission innovation based on the hydrostatic principle. The engine and wheels are hydraulically locked and full braking of the locomotive can be carried out using the engine as a brake. This feature increases the safety of the locomotive when used on conventional duties and gradients less than 1 in 15 and reduces the possibility of a skid when descending such gradients. Power comes from a flameproof Perkins diesel engine driving via a swash plate hydraulic transmission to either all four wheels for adhesion drive or two pinions for rack drive. In rack drive, the pinions engage an "Abt" type rack rigidly mounted between the rails. The tooth form of the rack is based on experience gained on the Snowdon Mountain Railway. The new locomotive is seen on test at Ledston Luck Colliery where a special track had been constructed incorporating gradients ranging from 1 in 10 to 1 in 4. *(National Coal Board)*

. . . and on the NCB

New wagon types

Prototypes of two important new freight wagon designs were completed by BREL during 1981. Vehicle type VGA, also known as a Full Side Access Van, has been developed to meet expanding requirements within BR's Speedlink network and features two sliding door panels on each side to give unrestricted access to the interior. Carrying capacity is 27 tonnes with a tare weight of 17·1 tonnes. Wheelbase is 9000mm (29ft 6½in).

Freightliner's prototype PFA four-axle 40ft container wagon was displayed for the first time at Railfreight 81 in March (see p44 & 45). Developed to match the growing use of deep-sea 40ft ISO containers, the vehicle is of skeletal design with a low tare weight of 11 tonnes and a payload capacity of 30 tonnes. Construction was carried out at BREL's Shildon facility. (Both: *BR via BREL*)

A rare visitor to Crewe Works in March was class 27 No 27203. This locomotive, following in the wake of class 26 No 26013, was sent to Crewe for thorough assessment by BR Design staff in preparation for the heavy general overhaul planned for class 26 and 27 locomotives. This work is to be put in hand at Glasgow Works. No 27203 stands at Gresty Lane, Crewe, on the morning of 17 March with class 85 No 85014, having arrived dead the previous night in the 1220 freight from Carlisle. *(Barry Nicolle)*

An interesting emu development took place at Crewe in the spring of 1981 when six class 303 units were transferred from Glasgow for introduction in June on Crewe-Liverpool services while class 304 and 310 units undergo refurbishment. Posing outside Crewe District Electric Traction Depot on 1 May 1981 are units 059 and 041. *(Barry Nicolle)*

Refurbishment of class 50s continued during 1981 at Doncaster Works and the accepted way of returning them to the WR was to run the locomotives light to York where they re-engined the 0940 Edinburgh-Plymouth. Here No 50033 *Glorious* waits at York on 16 October for the Deltic-hauled Plymouth train to arrive from Edinburgh. As from 2 November 1981, this train became a HST working, bringing an end to this convenient arrangement. *(Murray Brown)*

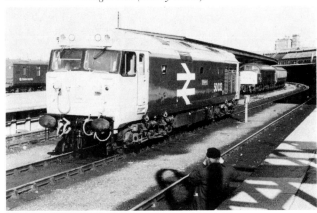

Off the beaten track

Class 40 No 40006 broke new ground for the class on 29 September when it double-headed the Ellesmere Port-Cranmore bitumen tanks throughout with class 25 No 25212. The duo were photographed after arrival at Cranmore with David Shepherd's Cranmore station as a backdrop. *(John Chalcraft)*

Photographers had an unexpected and, no doubt for some, unwanted bonus on 24 October 1981 whilst waiting for various steam specials on the Settle & Carlisle line. A BRB photographic special utilising a HST set surprised many onlookers, especially when it made numerous stops in photogenic spots. This was the second occasion that a HST set has been used for this purpose on this line. The special is pictured stationary on a bridge spanning the River Ribble at Batty Wood, just north of Stainforth. *(Brian Cooke)*.

In departmental use

The Departmental scene on BR is followed by many devotees and 1981 was a varied year for enthusiasts who find absorbing this aspect of BR operation. Departmental stock includes many 'vintage' vehicles which were formerly revenue earning and are in many instances the only surviving examples. At the same time the modern high performance railway calls for highly specialised purpose-built equipment.

On 1 February 1981, class 06 No 06003 was withdrawn from service at Dundee and shortly afterwards set off on its longest journey to date—to Reading. It was destined to receive Departmental No 97804 in readiness to take over duties in Reading signal works from Ruston & Hornsby 88hp 0-4-0 No 97020. Here is No 06003, having survived its epic journey from Dundee, resting at Reading. The date was 2 May 1981. *(Barry Nicolle)*

BR's sole surviving class 05 shunter, which is domiciled on the Isle of Wight, was given a new number in the 978XX series reserved for Departmental locomotives. It received the number 97803 in March, and in this guise was photographed at Sandown on 3 October 1981. *(Iain Whitlam)*

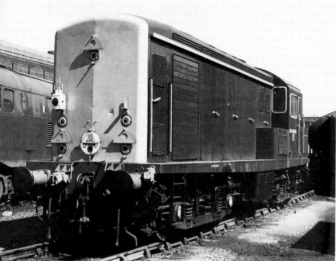

For some time the four former class 15 locomotives converted to stationary pre-heat vehicles were causing maintenance problems due to a lack of spares. Four class 31/0 "Toffee-apples" were duly converted to pre-heat units, forecasting the demise of the former class 15s. The first to be condemned was ADB 968003 (formerly No D8203) on 3 July 1981. ADB 968002, one of the three survivors, is pictured here in exemplary condition at Stratford on 15 April 1981. *(Barry Nicolle)*

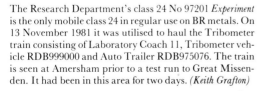

The Research Department's class 24 No 97201 *Experiment* is the only mobile class 24 in regular use on BR metals. On 13 November 1981 it was utilised to haul the Tribometer train consisting of Laboratory Coach 11, Tribometer vehicle RDB999000 and Auto Trailer RDB975076. The train is seen at Amersham prior to a test run to Great Missenden. It had been in this area for two days. *(Keith Grafton)*

The Speno SM775 rail corrugation recording vehicle paid a second visit to this country in July and August, 1981, covering approximately 1400 miles during rail assessment runs. The Swiss vehicle was photographed at Harwich after unloading. *(Ken Groom)*

Top right. Test Coach Iris was photographed at Beckenham Junction on 22 June during a visit to the South Eastern Division. The unit, which has radio antennas at each end, was gathering data in connection with the National Radio Plan. *(Brian Garvin)*

In 1981 the Civil Engineering Department took delivery from BREL of a new type of wagon, a bogie skip vehicle, and, continuing the long established theme of nautical nomenclature, bestowed on the type the name 'Skate'. There are 22 of these vehicles, numbered DB 997801-997822 with a TOPS code YDA. Each wagon weighs 26 tonnes and has a maximum speed of 45mph. DB997813 was on show at the Derby Litchurch Lane Works Open Day on 8 August. *(Keith Grafton)*

The last surviving Thompson CL (Composite Lavatory) coach on BR was broken up at Cambridge in early November. This vehicle was one of the last Thompson coaches to be built in 1953 and was of LNER Diagram 338. It survived in revenue service until June 1964 whereupon it was converted to Departmental use and renumbered DE 321046. When condemned in August 1981, the coach was still sporting its maroon livery and original number of E88519E. One other coach to Diagram 338 survives in preservation. DE 321046 was photographed at Cambridge on 13 October 1981. The former oval window, the Thompson 'trademark', can be seen in the middle of the vehicle. *(Barry Nicolle)*

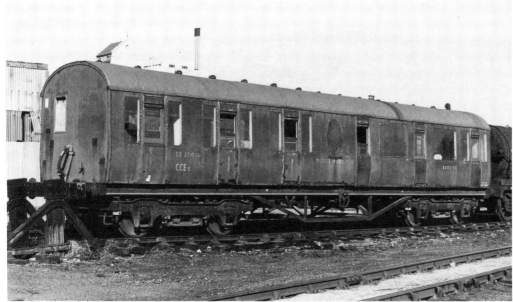

Class 25s Nos 25296 and 25308 arrive at Wellington (Salop) with the 1007SO Aberystwyth-Euston on 25 July 1981. Class 25s handle these summer trains over the Cambrian section, working through to Wolverhampton where electric traction takes over. *(Norman Preedy)*

Two of a kind

A familiar practice continued in 1981 by the LMR was the rostering of class 20s to work some of the East Coast trains from the Midlands. The 1258SO Skegness-Derby was photographed at the latter location on 5 September 1981 with Nos 20088 and 20157 in charge. *(Norman Preedy)*

From the introduction of the 1981 summer timetable, two WR class 31s were rostered to work the 0910SO Swansea-Portsmouth Harbour, a dated extension of the regular 1114 Bristol Temple Meads-Portsmouth Harbour. Two unidentified members of the class are seen on this duty near Codford on 22 August 1981. *(Dave Walden)*

The summer timetable saw regular double-heading of the 1038 Inverness-Aberdeen service. Class 27s Nos 27008 and 27105 accelerate away from Inverness on 25 June 1981. *(John Chalcraft)*

Another changing aspect of BR's rolling stock fleet affects freight vehicles. The generally depressed freight market in 1981 went some way towards accelerating BR's move away from unfitted and vacuum fitted goods vehicles. Unfitted mineral hoppers, so long part of the North Eastern scene and now being replaced by type HBA air-braked vehicles, form the major part of this train of condemned wagons seen at Tyne Yard on 22 June behind class 31 No 31289. *(Barry Nicolle)*

Made redundant

The decision by BR to withdraw from the C & D business (collection and delivery) in 1981 spelt the end of the line for several types of vehicle, including some built before the war. The Southern Region wooden bodied PMVs (Parcels & Miscellaneous Van) types NQV and NOV of the 13- and 14-ton varieties faced complete extinction, as did the former LMS 25-ton bogied NFV type vehicles numbered in the M31XXX series. However 25 of the Southern Region's wooden bodied NFVs numbered in the S2XX series are being retained for the Hastings line. BR CCTs (Covered Carriage Truck) numbered in the 941xx series were a little more fortunate: 500 are to be retained for residual traffic. Several of the 4-wheeled SR vans have been purchased for preservation and examples acquired in 1981 can be found on the Middleton, Shackerstone, and Kent & East Sussex Railways and also at the Southport Museum. Many of the LMS NFV bogied vehicles have also been given an extended life in Departmental use: 20 such vehicles have been allocated to BR's Paper & Printing section for conveyance of stationery.

NQV—Parcels & Miscellaneous Van (PMV)—No S1811 spent one day of its last year in service at York where it was pictured in April. This type of vehicle was due for extinction with the exception of a few sold for preservation. No S1811 has had a good life, having been built in 1942 at Lancing. *(Murray Brown)*

Built at Wolverton in 1944, NFV No M31220 is a former LMS B parcels van. Vehicles of this type run until shopping becomes due, when a decision is made as to their fate. This example was photographed at Cambridge on 24 November while forming part of the 0925MX non-passenger carrying coaching stock (NPCCS) working from Peterborough West Yard to Thornton Fields. *(Barry Nicolle)*

BR NETWORK

Woodhead slips away

Woodhead's last winter is recalled in this fine study of class 76 locomotives Nos 76012 and 76013 descending past Thurlestone with a westbound coal train on 11 February 1981. *(Les Nixon)*

On 23 March 1981, Nos 76023 and 76022 approach Dinting 'wrong line' due to a previous derailment which resulted in the Up line being disconnected at the east end of Dinting viaduct. Several minor incidents of this type affected operations in the final months. The Glossop branch is in the foreground. *(F A Blencowe)*

Electrification remained a major issue during 1981 with continuing discussions between BR and the Department of Transport eventually resulting in December in Government approval for the proposed extension of the GE catenary from Colchester to Harwich, Ipswich and Norwich. Substantial progress was also made with the Midland Suburban scheme in readiness for services in 1982 and small extensions to the West Coast network were made at Hazel Grove and Coatbridge. But it was the closure of an electrified line, the trans-Pennine Woodhead route which made the enthusiast headlines in 1981 and we begin this section with a cameo of this fascinating line. The Woodhead route finally closed on 18 July. The sections which closed completely were those between Penistone and Hadfield and the electrified Worsborough branch from Penistone to Wath. The main line from Penistone to Sheffield survived for use by the Sheffield-Penistone-Huddersfield passenger service as did the Manchester-Hadfield-Glossop section. It was intended to close the line on 1 June but BR gave a seven week reprieve to permit the railway unions to hold their own inconclusive inquiry into the closure under former ACAS Chairman Mr J E Mortimer.

The Worsborough branch was the first section to be de-wired following closure. Pictured descending Worsborough Bank and approaching Silkstone tunnels in July 1981 are Nos 76007 and 76012. *(Les Nixon)*

The closure of the freight only Woodhead route was noted for its lack of special trains in the final months, much to the chagrin of the enthusiast fraternity. Opponents of the closure pointed out that the line was frequently used as a diversionary route and 1981 witnessed this on several occasions. Here is a revenue earning passenger train using the line on 22 March with class 45/1 No 45101 approaching Crowden heading the diverted 0746 St Pancras-Manchester. *(Les Nixon)*

The barren but photogenic nature of the Woodhead route is illustrated in this picture of a three-car BRCW dmu forming a BR inspection train approaching Crowden on 8 July 1981. On the following day, the line was washed out at this point, almost causing premature closure. *(Les Nixon)*

Last rites on the Worsborough branch. Immediately following closure, dewiring commenced on this section and was expected to take six months to complete. Class 20 Nos 20209 and 20093 approach Wombwell Main Junction on 29 October 1981 with a train that says it all. The wires from this section have already been removed. *(Les Nixon)*

In despair there is hope. Whilst closure of the Woodhead route was being mourned, other routes were receiving the residual traffic. A BOC block train heads up the Hope Valley towards Sheffield on 28 July 1981. Until closure, this was one of the regular trains to use the Woodhead route. *(Les Nixon)*

A slab track paving machine in use at the new Kings Cross Midland interchange station. Some 2km of track in tunnels will consist of concrete paved track at a level lower than the old conventional track to give required clearances for overhead line equipment. The line to Moorgate, which diverges from the Bedford-St Pancras route at Dock Junction, north of St Pancras, will be known as the Midland City Line. The tipper vehicle on the right is discharging ready-mixed concrete into the paving machine. The photograph was taken on 9 March 1981. *(BR LMR)*

Service disruption is inevitable during electrification programmes with some inconvenience to the customer. The LMR has taken pains to alleviate this burden by regularly issuing progress reports as work proceeds and has also made use of posters such as this example indicating progress as at 30 September 1981. *(BR LMR)*

MSE *progress*

BR's main electrification project in 1981 was the continuing programme of work on the Bedford-St Pancras line, already christened the 'Bed-Pan' line! The scheme, which includes new and reconstructed stations, resignalling and new rolling stock, is officially dubbed the MSE—Midland Suburban Electrification. This selection of photographs portrays some of the changing scenes and the magnitude of the MSE scheme.

The changing scene on the Midland line. The remains of Finchley Road signal box were demolished shortly after this photograph was taken on 27 July 1981. Soon the dmu will also be part of the past at this location. *(Brian Cooke)*

Rolling stock for the MSE takes the form of the newly designed class 317 emus, 48 of which are being constructed at BREL's York and Derby Litchurch Lane facilities. Two sets are seen at the recently built depot at Cricklewood on 10 October 1981 following delivery the previous evening. The two four-car units, Nos 317 301 and 317 302, are at this point still coupled to the brake vans which have served as barrier vehicles during transit. *(Keith Grafton)*

In this later view of the Kings Cross Midland interchange, taken on 8 May, the concrete paved track is in position and work is well advanced on the platform canopy steelwork. *(BR LMR)*

The first section of the MSE scheme to be energised was between Bedford and Luton Hoo. Power was switched on from 12 January 1981 using a supply taken from the CEGB national grid via this feeder station at Sundon, north of Luton. A similar installation at Graham Park, Mill Hill, provides power for the southern end of the scheme. *(BR LMR)*

The prime interest in this picture taken at Cricklewood on 24 April appears to be the HST, the 0730 Leeds-Kings Cross diverted to St Pancras due to a derailment between Newark and Grantham. However, two days later Cricklewood Junction box and its associated semaphore signals were taken out of use as the fifth stage of the London-Irchester resignalling was commissioned. A later view on 22 October at the same location shows the local line tracks re-aligned for 75mph running instead of the previous 25mph (Both: *BR LMR*)

Station modernisation is an important feature of the MSE scheme and rebuilt passenger facilities were already in use at Bedford and Radlett at the beginning of 1981. During the year station reconstruction at Hendon was also completed. These two photographs were taken on 3 October and show the confident exterior and the light interior, where one member of staff issues tickets and controls access to and from the platforms by means of a treadle-operated turnstile. (Both: *BR LMR*)

Under the wires at Hazel Grove . . .

An extension to an existing electrified system took place on 1 June 1981 when 2½ route miles were brought into use between Stockport and Hazel Grove. The £1·1m scheme was financed by the Greater Manchester PTE, much of the cost being for altering overbridges to give accepted clearances and for providing a new footbridge at Hazel Grove. The latter is seen in this view of a terminating service from Altrincham on 18 July 1981. Recast electric services between Altrincham-Alderley Edge and Crewe provided the units to work the extension. *(Tom Heavyside)*

Further north, an important section of newly electrified line was formally opened on 11 August 1981 by Mr Roderick Macleod, Chairman of the Scottish Railway Board and member of the BRB. Energising at 25kV the 7km section linking the major Freightliner Terminal at Coatbridge to the electrified West Coast Main Line at Mossend Yard dispensed with the need to change traction at Mossend for the short distance to Coatbridge. The work took nine months to complete and cost £930,000, 30% of which was met by a grant from the European Regional Development Fund. Balfour Beatty undertook the works, which required 261 overhead structures. In the picture, a Freightliner leaves the Coatbridge terminal shortly after the official opening hauled by two electric locomotives, led by No 81020. *(BR Glasgow)*

. . . and at Coatbridge

International connections

Sir Peter Parker, BRB Chairman, officially opened new passenger facilities at Gatwick station on 9 July 1981. The station is undergoing a two stage development, the first of which was the provision of a new streamlined passenger concourse built on a raft above the six platforms. The concourse contains a travel centre and ticket office and is served by escalators. Then under construction was the second stage which incorporates the installation of a footbridge with escalators and stairs to give direct access to the airport's departure lounge. Completion was expected by late 1982 at an estimated cost of £11m. (BR Waterloo)

On 31 May 1981 Sealink successfully introduced a Jetfoil service between Dover and Ostend for which SR introduced special connecting services from and to Victoria. Here the *Prinses Stephanie* makes for the Belgian coast on 2 August after leaving its special berthing pontoon located between Dover's main quay and the train ferry dock. (Brian Garvin)

At Dover Western Docks station, this new footbridge provides a link for Jetfoil passengers between the platform and the new reception area opened for this service. (Brian Garvin)

Selby diversion takes shape

Construction continued during 1981 of the Selby Diversion line, which is being built to divert the East Coast main line away from the Selby Coalfield. The new line is 23·5km long and will leave the present ECML at Temple Hirst near mile post 169, pass under the Leeds-Selby line at Hambleton and join the York-Sheffield and Leeds lines at Colton near the 5¼ mile post. This January 1981 picture shows the new line at Hambleton, intersection with the Leeds-Selby line. The view is looking north towards York and shows the formations of the curves connecting the two routes. *(BR York)*

This was the scene at Temple Hirst, southern junction with the present ECML, on 19 May 1981. Class 55 No 55010 is crossing the River Aire with the 1415 York-Kings Cross. The new diversionary line will cross from left to right to join the ECML. Initial piling works can be seen on the river bank. *(Stephen Bellamy)*

This late 1981 view *(bottom right)* of the site of Colton Junction shows track ballast and signalling relay rooms already in position, while a WR class 253 unit heads away from the camera towards York on a service from the West Country. Both junctions at Colton and Temple Hirst are intended to allow 125mph working. *(BR ER)*

Taken at the southern end of the diversion looking north, this autumn 1981 picture shows three of the new bridges necessitated by the new line. The nearest carries the A19 Selby-Doncaster road. *(BR ER)*

Almost 14 years to the day since it closed, Dronfield station was reopened on 5 January 1981. The new station and service are the result of close co-operation between BR and two councils, Derbyshire County and North East Derbyshire District, who have provided £90,000 to rebuild the station and transform the goods yard into a car park for 50 vehicles. Each platform has a stone waiting shelter built from sandstone recovered from disused buildings at Penistone to blend with local surroundings. Sir Peter Parker attended the opening ceremony watched by over 200 school children waving flags in time with the Ireland Colliery Junior Band. A 6-car dmu worked a Dronfield-Sheffield-Dronfield excursion in connection with the reopening. *(Les Nixon)*

Stations new and not so new

Exterior and interior views of Kensal Green station on the Euston-Watford dc electric line which was opened in January 1981 after complete rebuilding at a cost of £250,000. BR architects at Euston designed the new building which includes a travel office and staff accommodation. A distinctive feature is a natural wood trussed roof. Councillor Bill McLellan, Mayor of Brent, opened the station which is used by ¾m passengers annually. The London Divisional Manager, Harry Reed, considered the old station the worst of all the 108 stations in the Division, dating from LNWR days and still sporting LMS colours! (Both: *BR Euston*)

Birchwood Station
Opened by
Sir Peter Parker MVO
Chairman, British Railways Board
31st July 1981

A new station at Birchwood, situated between Padgate and Glazebrook on the Liverpool-Manchester line, was opened by Sir Peter Parker on 31 July 1981. The station cost £¾m and was a joint venture involving BR, Warrington Borough Council, Warrington New Town Development Corporation and local bus operators. The latter have provided good interchange facilities and the public are offered over 50 trains each day. Pleasing design is a feature of this new station, especially the footbridge. On 10 October 1981, the 1512 Warrington Central-Manchester Piccadily led by No M51913 rolls to a stop. A plaque commemorating the opening is fixed to the building. (Both: *Tom Heavyside*)

Honeybourne station on the Oxford-Worcester line was reopened to passengers on 22 May 1981. The station was closed on 5 May 1969 and efforts to have the station reconnected to the network were led by the Cotswold Line Promotion Group. Honeybourne has doubled in size since 1969 and BR felt that there was now passenger potential. The re-opening was also supported by the Hereford and Worcester County Council and the Wyehaven District Council. The 1140 Worcester-Paddington train hauled by class 47/4 No 47510 *Fair Rosamund* with special headboard was the first to stop and was greeted by several local groups including schoolchildren. Mr Ronald Carrington, Chairman of the County Council's Strategic Planning & Transportation Committee declared the station open by flagging away the train. *(BR Bristol)*

Passengers returned to the station at Bolsover, Derbyshire, on 16 August when class 47/3 No 47316 took a charter excursion to Skegness. Although this was not the first time Bolsover has seen special passenger traffic, scheduled services ended in July 1930. Formerly a MR line linking Staveley Town and Mansfield Woodhouse (Pleasley Jct), the truncated section from Staveley (Seymour Jct) to Bolsover survives to serve Markham Colliery and the Bolsover Coalite plant.
No 47316 here enters the station from the Glapwell end after running round its train. *(Les Nixon)*

A new joint service was inaugurated on 24 June 1981 between BR, the National Bus Company and Humberside County Council to improve journey times across the River Humber following the opening of the new road bridge and cessation of the ferry service between Hull and New Holland. Barton on Humber became the focal point of this venture and an hourly service is now provided with integrated bus and train services. On the opening day, the picture shows from left to right David Price, BR Area Terminals Manager, Immingham, Ken Hobson, BR Divisional PRO, Doncaster, Julie Shaw, BR, Doncaster, Mrs N Stephenson, Chairman, Humberside County Council, Ken Taylor, BR Divisional Manager, Doncaster, and John Reeves, Area Manager, Immingham. The symbolic oversize ticket indicates a cost of £2.36 for the complete single journey from Cleethorpes to Hull. *(BR Eastern Region)*

Last trains

A 6-car dmu formed the last train on the Rawtenstall branch on 14 February 1981. The line lost its passenger service on 5 June 1972 but remained open for freight until 4 December 1980. The East Lancashire Railway Preservation Society are endeavouring to re-open the Rossendale Valley line and restore passenger services again to Rawtenstall. No M50505, the end vehicle of the last special, is pictured at Bury Bolton Street station during a stop to permit participants to visit the Bury Transport Museum. *(Tom Heavyside)*

May 1981 saw the closure of two short branches, both of which were host to farewell dmu specials. In Scotland on 2 May 1981 was closed the Brechin branch, the surviving remnant of the former Caledonian route to the south via Forfar and Perth which closed to passengers in 1967. The closure also meant the end of the famous Kinnaber Junction (as a junction—the main Dundee-Aberdeen line through this point, of course, survives), forever remembered as the meeting point of the East and West Coast routes in the Railway Races in 1895. A 3-car dmu special was run from Edinburgh and this was strengthened at Dundee by single vehicle No SC55000. The last train is seen in Brechin station which was decorated for the occasion by the Brechin Railway Preservation Society. This group has set its sights on saving initially the four-mile section from Brechin to Bridge of Dun with the eventual hope of continuing to Montrose. *(Colin Sykes)*

The Wallingford branch, which ran from Cholsey on the GWR main line near Didcot, was closed on 31 May 1981 with a BR dmu tour, 'The Wallingford Wanderer'. The branch lost its passenger services in June 1959 but will be remembered for the steam jollifications which took place using preserved locomotives from the Great Western Society's Didcot depot. Freight traffic to the Associated British Maltings Ltd's siding continued until 29 May 1981, when No 31131 worked the final freight. It is pictured collecting the last two wagons for ABM's siding. *(T W Harper)*

A closure which took place on 30 May 1981 received little mention. However, this was to be expected for eventually the line in question, the South Shields branch, is to become part of the Tyne & Wear Metro system at an estimated cost of £280m. Past memories are relived with this photograph of a six-car dmu at South Shields forming the 1700 from Newcastle in the spring of 1981. *(Peter Robinson)*

Another Tyneside closure proposal which will probably generate little criticism was announced by BR in July. This concerned the section of line between Newcastle West Junction and Blaydon Junction via the Scotswood bridge. Carlisle-bound trains leave Newcastle Central and stay on the north side of the river Tyne before crossing the river by the Scotswood bridge to Blaydon and thence to Hexham and Carlisle. Under the closure proposal trains would leave Newcastle and immediately cross the Tyne via the King Edward bridge before traversing the current freight only route via Norwood junction and Dunston and then regaining the present line to Carlisle at Blaydon. The doomed Scotswood bridge is being crossed here by the 1508 Newcastle-Hexham two-car dmu on 28 September 1981. *(Peter Robinson)*

Tyneside closures

The section of the former GNR/GER Joint line between Spalding and March has been proposed for closure. This famous line, still known by railwaymen as the 'Joint', is a shadow of its former self and BR feels that the small amount of existing traffic can be accommodated on the March-Peterborough-Spalding line. Many level crossings make this section of the 'Joint' particularly expensive to operate and this has contributed to the closure notice. *(Murray Brown)*

Under threat

In 1981 the news broke that possibly the most famous viaduct in the country, Batty Moss at Ribblehead, was seemingly not so permanent as was believed. The Divisional Civil Engineer at BR Preston, in whose area Ribblehead is situated, in the last ten years has spent £¾m on upkeep but deterioration is increasing at a rapid pace. Its exposed position to the Pennine weather has finally taken its toll and severe cracking caused by freezing damp and rain has been increasingly evident in recent years. BR has intimated that it would be cheaper to construct a replacement as opposed to repairing the viaduct, but the cost of a new structure has been estimated at some £6m. With the contraction of services using the line, BR is having to decide if it has a future as a through route. The S & C has become a classic steam route and should closure take place such stirring scenes as 'Black Fives' Nos 4767 and 5407 crossing Ribblehead viaduct on 4 April 1981 will become all too sadly a memory. *(Ted Parker)*

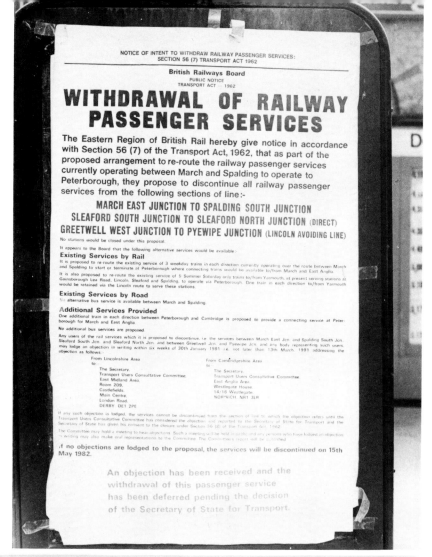

NOTICE OF INTENT TO WITHDRAW RAILWAY PASSENGER SERVICES:
SECTION 56 (7) TRANSPORT ACT 1962

British Railways Board
PUBLIC NOTICE
TRANSPORT ACT — 1962

WITHDRAWAL OF RAILWAY PASSENGER SERVICES

The Eastern Region of British Rail hereby give notice in accordance with Section 56 (7) of the Transport Act, 1962, that as part of the proposed arrangement to re-route the railway passenger services currently operating between March and Spalding to operate to Peterborough, they propose to discontinue all railway passenger services from the following sections of line:-

MARCH EAST JUNCTION TO SPALDING SOUTH JUNCTION
SLEAFORD SOUTH JUNCTION TO SLEAFORD NORTH JUNCTION (DIRECT)
GREETWELL WEST JUNCTION TO PYEWIPE JUNCTION (LINCOLN AVOIDING LINE)

No stations would be closed under this proposal.

It appears to the Board that the following alternative services would be available:-

Existing Services by Rail
It is proposed to re-route the existing service of 3 weekday trains in each direction currently operating over the route between March and Spalding to start or terminate at Peterborough where connecting trains would be available to/from March and East Anglia.

It is also proposed to re-route the existing service of 5 Summer Saturday only trains to/from Yarmouth, at present serving stations at Gainsborough Lea Road, Lincoln, Sleaford and Spalding, to operate via Peterborough. One train in each direction to/from Yarmouth would be retained via the Lincoln route to serve these stations.

Existing Services by Road
No alternative bus service is available between March and Spalding.

Additional Services Provided
One additional train in each direction between Peterborough and Cambridge is proposed to provide a connecting service at Peterborough for March and East Anglia.

No additional bus services are proposed.

Any users of the rail services which it is proposed to discontinue, i.e. the services between March East Jcn. and Spalding South Jcn. Sleaford South Jcn. and Sleaford North Jcn. and between Greetwell Jcn. and Pyewipe Jcn. and any body representing such users, may lodge an objection in writing within six weeks of 30th January 1981 i.e. not later than 13th March 1981 addressing the objection as follows:

From Lincolnshire Area | From Cambridgeshire Area
to | to
The Secretary, | The Secretary,
Transport Users Consultative Committee, | Transport Users Consultative Committee,
East Midland Area, | East Anglia Area,
Room 209, | Westgate House,
Castlefields, | 14/16 Westgate,
Main Centre, | NORWICH. NR1 3LR
London Road, |
DERBY. DE1 2PE |

If any such objection is lodged, the services cannot be discontinued from the section of line to which the objection refers until the Transport Users Consultative Committee has considered the objection and reported to the Secretary of State for Transport and the Secretary of State has given his consent to the closure under Section 56 (8) of the Transport Act, 1962.

The Committee may hold a meeting to hear objections. Such a meeting will be held in public and any persons who have lodged an objection in writing may also make oral representations to the Committee. The Committee's report will be published.

If no objections are lodged to the proposal, the services will be discontinued on 15th May 1982.

An objection has been received and the withdrawal of this passenger service has been deferred pending the decision of the Secretary of State for Transport.

Barmouth Bridge reopens

Barmouth viaduct reopened to traffic on 22 May 1981 following seven months of closure and £500,000 of expenditure on initial repairs after the discovery that a marine woodworm had caused serious damage to the wooden piles. Machynlleth driver Neville Pritchard drove the first train the 1042 Shrewsbury-Pwllheli, over the reopened bridge. The inaugural train is seen leaving Morfa Mawddach immediately south of the bridge. *(BR LMR)*

An impression of the magnitude of the work necessary to repair or replace the wooden piles of the bridge can be clearly gained from this picture as the 1240 Shrewsbury-Pwllheli crosses on 22 June 1981. *(Tom Heavyside)*

New facilities

Improvements at Eastfield depot, Glasgow, include a new fuel dispensing point which came into use during 1981. All services are provided through hoses suspended on trolley rails for ease of handling. Class 37 No 37112 leads the queue one day in September. *(Colin Boocock)*

Sir Julian Ridsdale, MP for Harwich, declared open the new £2m Clacton emu depot on 17 July 1981. The three-road depot can accommodate three 4-car emus and will be responsible for maintaining 66 vehicles of four different classes. *(Keith Grafton)*

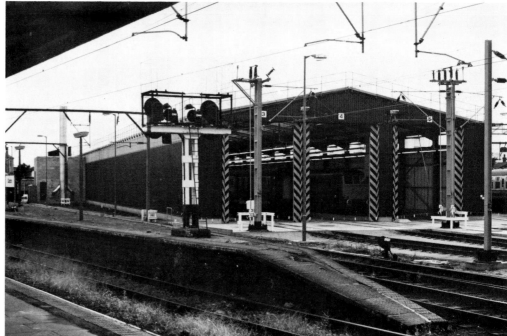

The familiar outline at the top right hand corner of the photograph betrays the location as Plymouth, where a new £7m facility at Laira depot was officially opened on 30 September 1981 by the Lord Mayor of Plymouth, Councillor Ralph Morrell. Expansion of the 20-year old depot to cater for the 18 HST units destined for Scotland— North-East — South-West services began at the end of 1978 when a Truro firm, E Thomas & Co Ltd, was awarded the contract. The 240m long workshop contains three tracks and handles locomotive-hauled coaching stock as well as HST vehicles. The photograph also depicts the ten new stabling sidings provided in the improvement scheme. *(BR WR)*

Improved facilities for the maintenance of Scottish Region's dmu fleet include this new servicing depot at Corkerhill, Glasgow, opened in 1981. *(Colin Boocock)*

Tyne and Wear Metro progress

The Queen officially opened the Tyne & Wear Metro on 6 November, riding a 'Super Tram' over the latest section completed, from Haymarket to Heworth. On the same occasion Her Majesty opened the bridge bearing her name which carries the Metro 82ft above the Tyne. Extending from Forth Banks on the Newcastle side to Greensfield, next to BR's Gateshead depot, the 540ft span bridge is the sixth to link the city with Gateshead. Here a pre-opening train for Heworth, headed by car No 4039, crosses the new bridge on 25 October. *(Peter Robinson)*

One of BR's successes in 1981 was an expansion of its Speedlink network of wagon load traffic using fast air-braked services. The introduction of new air-braked vehicles of many varying types to accommodate different traffics together with the enormous benefits of the BR TOPS computer system has contributed to ensuring that Speedlink is here to stay. Whilst the recession in 1981 brought about a reduction in tonnage, there was no loss of business to the roads and the forecast for 1982 was a 75% increase over 1981 figures. Over 60 Speedlink trains a day were running by the end of 1981 and the short transit times provided by this service have meant that it is not just the bulk commodities that are suitable for rail travel but also many smaller traffics. A mixed Speedlink train hauled by an unidentified class 37 approaches York from the south in July 1981. *(Roger Bastin)*

Changing face of BR freight

Development of the Speedlink network in 1981 has led to a steady increase in the number of Polybulk wagons in use in East Anglia for the movement of grain. With a gross laden weight of 80 tonnes, these bogie air-braked hoppers are replacing the conventional 20·5 tonne four-wheeled vacuum-braked and unfitted wagons used hitherto. Polybulk vehicles are loaded at Bury St Edmunds, Chettisham, Newmarket and Whittlesford on the Norwich Division to be worked forward in Speedlink services to places such as Dover and Birkenhead.

Here class 37 No 37089 leaves Newmarket grain depot for Cambridge yard on 16 October with a control special comprising four loaded Polybulks and a brake van. *(Barry Nicolle)*

Vast improvements to rail travellers will result from commissioning of the Victoria signalling centre at Clapham Junction. GEC-General Signal is the main contractor and the new box includes a microcomputer-based train describer system which is being introduced in parallel with the resignalling. Eventually the 51 miles of the Victoria-Brighton main line will be controlled from two boxes—Victoria and Three Bridges. The developments are part of a major £120m track improvement and resignalling programme inaugurated in 1978. When the scheme is completed, some 270 track miles will be under the control of the centre and over 70 existing signal boxes will have disappeared. The photographs show internal and external views of the new signalling centre. (Both: *Steve Robb*)

Victoria signalling centre

Resignalling at Salisbury . . .

The £2m Salisbury resignalling scheme controlled from a new panel in Salisbury station was commissioned during 17-21 August 1981. In all 82½ miles of track are under the supervision of this power box which is intended to link up with the Eastleigh box in 1982. The Salisbury scheme has meant the end of eight manual boxes and the area embraced by the new panel extends to Grately on the Andover line, Dean on the Romsey line and Wilton on the main line westwards. 1982 will see the area extended to include Upton Lovell on the Westbury line, Dunbridge on the Romsey route and westwards towards Gillingham. The new Laverstock curve (see opposite) can be seen on the panel immediately above the telephone on the right of the picture. *(BR Waterloo)*

The switchover to the new panel at Salisbury brought an end to the low pressure electro-pneumatically operated semaphore system installed by the LSWR in the early part of the century. These two views show the lever frame in the old Salisbury West box and the diagram from Salisbury East. The lever frame from the former installation is being preserved by the NRM. *(Both: Dave Walden)*

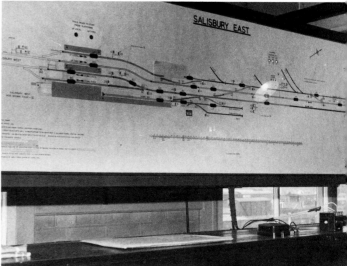

The new scheme included reinstatement of a ⅜-mile section which has been out of use as a through route since 1859! The new line, known as the Laverstock Loop, completes the triangle between the Basingstoke-Salisbury and the Southampton/Romsey-Salisbury lines and provides an alternative route between Basingstoke and Southampton. Extensive renewals are planned on the main line between Southampton and Basingstoke and future diverted trains will be able to proceed to Salisbury and then use the new spur to gain their destination. Royal Assent for restoration of the line was given in July 1981. Apart from clearing the undergrowth, an underbridge needed repairing but the new line was opened in 2 months after commencement of the work. Initial reinstatement work is evident in the picture on the left while on the right is the first train to use the line, a class 33 hauled 3-coach test train, which ran on 28 August 1981. The train is facing south towards Romsey. On the left can be seen the line leading into Salisbury whilst out of sight at the back of the photograph is the Salisbury-Waterloo main line. *(Dave Walden, BR Waterloo)*

. . . *and at Southampton*

The colour light signal in the foreground foreshadows the end of Southampton's famous signal gantry. The Southampton area resignalling scheme is controlled from a new electronic panel in Eastleigh signal box and the switchover on 9 November brought to an end this familiar sight at Southampton. This area was the third stage of the scheme and completed the link with Basingstoke. Completion of the scheme in October 1982 will bring the entire main line from Waterloo to the Hampshire coast under the control of colour light signals. Class 423 4VEP No 7839 passes under the gantry on 18 August 1981 with the 1442 Waterloo-Bournemouth. *(Tom Heavyside)*

South Eastern Division changes

Following BR's withdrawal from the C & D parcels business, the once large depot and sidings at Bricklayers Arms closed on 1 June 1981. The bleakness of the scene at this location is apparent in this study taken earlier in the year of class 33 No 33063 preparing to leave for Grain with oil empties from Salfords after running round its train. *(Brian Garvin)*

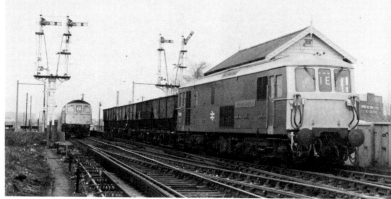

Access to Bricklayers Arms was controlled by this impressive box at North Kent West Junction. The box is seen again in this spring 1981 view of class 73/1 No 73101 *Brighton Evening Argus* leaving the yards with the 1012 trip working to Beckenham Junction coal concentration depot, a duty which originates from Acton since the closure of Bricklayers Arms. *(Brian Garvin)*

Closed earlier in 1981 due to the recession, the branch to Tilmanstone colliery in Kent was later re-opened when supplies of coal from Poland became uncertain owing to that country's internal difficulties. Initially coal from the line was moved to north-east England but this traffic later originated from Betteshanger, leaving Tilmanstone to supply local Kentish needs. In this photograph taken on 2 August at Shepherd's Well, junction of the branch with the Faversham-Dover line, Class 33 No 33051 has just returned from Tilmanstone with a ballast train and stands beside a withdrawn class 4SUB. This particular unit had been in use on the branch for a fire fighting exercise. *(Brian Garvin)*

By October 1981 good progress was being made with the first phase of the Westbury (Wilts) resignalling scheme. This new power box is being built at the north end of Westbury station on the Berks and Hants curve. Completion of the structure was expected by late 1982, following which existing semaphores in the Westbury area were to be eventually eliminated together with associated manual signal boxes *(Derek Short)*

From 16 May 1981 the ex-LSWR main line between Salisbury and a location east of Sherborne station passed back to SR control, while most of the attractive Westbury-Salisbury line was transferred from the SR to the WR. The photograph shows class 47 No 47230 leaving Warminster station on the latter line with the 1100 Bristol Temple Meads-Portsmouth Harbour on the day of the changeover. *(Ken Harris)*

WR developments

Modernisation in the Welsh Valleys. Early morning on 29 October 1981 at Park Junction, Newport and class 37 No 37248 comes down from the Western Valley with a train of empty ballast wagons whilst the S&T men prepare for a day's work. By mid-November the semaphore signalling had disappeared from this scene and the lines to Ebbw Vale controlled by colour light signals. *(Derek Short)*

The Cardiff Division of BR singled the Rhondda Fawr line between Porth and Treherbert and the single track timetable commenced on 30 March 1981. Previously 20 daily trains were run and the singling resulted in the loss of one, although the 0745 from Treherbert was combined with another train so that the same number of seats were provided. A sum of £175,000 was earmarked for new track and signalling at Porth and approximately £200,000 was also destined to be spent on track renewal on the remaining single line between Porth and Treherbert, an indication of BR's policy of safeguarding the Rhondda line by economising and investing where appropriate. The photograph depicts Dinas Rhondda on 29 June 1981 with the 1300 Barry Island-Treherbert approaching the camera 'wrong line', the train traversing the former up line. *(Tom Heavyside)*

As an experiment prior to giving selected class 37s names appropriate to the West Highland line, No 37027 was given an all-yellow nose and black cab window surrounds, making its debut at the Glasgow Works Open Day on 27 June. It was later decided that this livery was not to be adopted in general. Later in the year this locomotive was named *Loch Eil*. *(Colin Boocock)*

Open doors

BR staged several open days at its depots during 1981 and, as usual, provided a wide range of attractions, although at least one such event lacked publicity, resulting in poor attendance. However, most attracted large numbers, giving BR an excellent opportunity to show off its latest developments and offering visitors the chance to see traction units away from their usual habitats. Particularly refreshing was the continuing change of attitude in allowing privately owned steam locomotives to participate at these events.

Stratford depot's Open Day on 11 July provided the 'usual unusual' gathering of locomotives which, in the case of Stratford, is fairly easy to arrange as LMR, SR and WR locomotives are near at hand. One of the line-ups included newly named No 47158 *Henry Ford*, class 50 No 50036 *Victorious* and class 55 No 55021 *Argyll and Sutherland Highlander*. *(John Chalcraft)*

It is not every day that the public may ride behind a class 03 shunter but BR provided this opportunity at Barrow Hill, Staveley when the depot opened its doors on 4 October. No 03189, decorated with a railtour headboard, obliges. *(John Chalcraft)*

An open day was held at the new Clacton emu depot on 18 July 1981, the day after the official opening. On view were class 313 emu No 313034 alongside class 309 'Clacton' emu No 612. Also present on loan from the LMR was class 86/2 No 86244, a pointer for the future Anglia electrification approved in December. (Both: *Keith Grafton*)

Warrington welcomed visitors at the Central goods depot on 10 October 1981. Class 40 No 40115 leads the line-up of exhibits. Note the magnificent goods depot formerly belonging to the Cheshire Lines Committee and sporting its connections with the Midland, Great Central and Great Northern Railways. (*Tom Heavyside*)

The view at Old Oak Common depot on 20 September. The WR had provided a steam hauled shuttle service between Paddington Station and the depot with GWR Castle No 5051 and BR class 9F No 92220, the former visible in the foreground. (*Keith Grafton*)

BR TRAFFIC

Cardiff-Bristol-Portsmouth service improvements

Introduction of the 1981 timetable changes on 1 June witnessed major service improvements on the Cardiff-Bristol-Portsmouth route. Service frequency on weekdays was increased from two-hourly to hourly and additional through trains to and from Cardiff were provided. Motive power in the form of Eastleigh-based class 33s remained unchanged, as evident in this view of No 33106 drifting down Ashley Down bank into Bristol with a Cardiff-Portsmouth working on 9 July. *(John Chalcraft)*

Changes on the Weymouth line

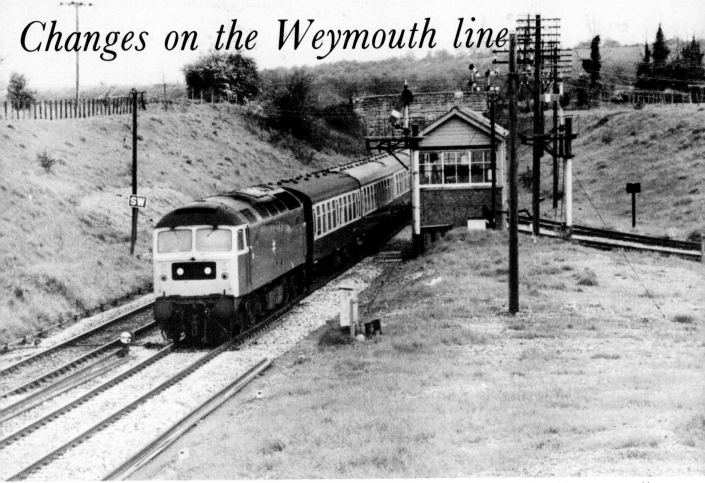

In connection with recasting of Cardiff-Bristol-Portsmouth services from 1 June, all but two of the former seven through weekday passenger workings from Bristol or Cardiff to Weymouth were discontinued, services instead being provided by dmus originating from Westbury to connect with Portsmouth line trains. One casualty of this change was the 0905 Cardiff-Weymouth which became a summer Saturdays only service. It is seen here behind class 47/0 No 47119 at Hawkeridge on 16 May, shortly before the new timetable took effect. *(Ken Harris)*

Regular revenue-earning passenger traffic returned to the previously freight only Thingley Junction (Chippenham)-Bradford Junction line on 13 July when BR initiated a Mondays to Thursdays 3-car dmu from Swindon to form up at Westbury with the 0910 dmu for Weymouth. The unit returned as part of the 1800 Weymouth-Bristol Temple Meads, going forward from Westbury to Swindon at 1955. The train was such a success that during the early part of the following week it was strengthened to six cars and from 30 July ran as locomotive and coaches, continuing in this form until 10 October. In this view taken at Bradford Junction on 28 July the driver of the evening return working is seen accepting the token for the single line to Thingley Junction. *(Dave Walden)*

Avon Link

WR's Bristol Division made an energetic and commendable promotion drive on the Severn Beach line commencing on 22 June 1981. The package included a new identity for the line—Avon Link—and a simplified fare structure of 20p, 40p or 60p single fares only. The single car dmu units carried the Avon Link motif and 10,000 copies of a promotional brochure were distributed to the residential areas around the line's stations. In October, the BRE-Leyland railbus NoRDB977020 arrived at Bristol and, following crew training, entered service on the Avon Link on 20 October 1981. Some slight difficulties were experienced with the operation of track circuits and at one stage, the railbus was to have been withdrawn and returned to Derby but following high level discussions, the vehicle remained on the service and provision was made for the driver to telephone the Bristol signal centre when the vehicle entered track circuited routes. Considerable interest has been generated by the railbus and, indeed, with the overall marketing effort passenger traffic has increased. The railbus was also utilised on an evening return service to Weston-Super-Mare. It is seen here calling at Clifton Down on 2 November while working the 1217 Severn Beach-Bristol. Note the 'Avon Link' motif with the station name picture. (Both: *John Chalcraft*)

The 'Avon Link' symbol is apparent adjacent to the double arrow symbols on No W55033, more regular motive power on the Severn Beach line. This view of the 1217 Severn Beach-Bristol Temple Meads was taken at Avonmouth on 14 November. (*John Chalcraft*)

Up for the Cup . . .

Manchester City met Tottenham Hotspur in the 1981 Centenary FA Cup Final on 9 May. In a year which also marked the 150th anniversary of the birth of George Pullman it was appropriate that both Manchester Pullman sets should be used to convey City officials and guests to the game. One of these workings, the 1108 Manchester Piccadilly-Wembley Central, is seen here at speed south of Crewe headed by class 83 No 83010. The match was drawn but Spurs emerged 3-2 victors from the replay! *(Barry Nicolle)*

. . . and down for the Open

For the 1981 Open Golf Championship at Sandwich the SR ran several extra trains between 16 and 19 July. One especially interesting working from Victoria on each of these days was locomotive-hauled and all first class using a LMR set of FOs and two of the remaining full kitchen cars. Fully sold out on each day, the train was principally patronised by business houses. Class 33 No 33056 *The Burma Star* provided the motive power on three days and is pictured passing Beckenham Junction on the outward run on 19 July. The third and eighth vehicles are kitchen cars. Other additional services provided in connection with this event were formed by emus. Local trains were also strengthened. *(Brian Garvin)*

Freightliner superpower

Additional loading of the daily Cardiff-Glasgow Freightliner from the start of the summer timetable necessitated increased power. Photographed in July, the early morning down train crosses the River Usk bridge on the northern outskirts of Newport hauled by two Cardiff Canton based class 47 locomotives led by No 47324. Other pairings noted on this duty included class 37 and class 47 combinations, but by October the train was powered by a single class 56. *(Derek Short)*

Another Freightliner service which attracted regular double heading in 1981 was the 1358 Tilbury-Garston, which also conveys portions for Trafford Park and Aintree. With 30 vehicles grossing up to 1850 tonnes, the train is booked for haulage by two class 37s from Tilbury to Willesden, where a pair of ac electric locomotives take over. Two views of this heavy train show Nos 37245 and 37246 storming the incline approaching Hampstead Heath station on 17 November and, on 20 July, a pair of class 85s in the shape of Nos 85022 and 85031 passing Carpenders Park, near Watford. *(Keith Grafton, Ken Harris)*

Deep and crisp and even

There is not much snow in evidence in this picture taken at Cambridge Coldham Lane depot on 9 December, but behind No 37023 S & T staff are grappling in sub-zero temperatures with the partially frozen bracket signal. A Cravens 2-car dmu passes forming the 1023 Peterborough-Cambridge. *(Barry Nicolle)*

For most of December much of Great Britain shivered under successive snowfalls and severely low temperatures. Inevitable disruption to BR services occurred but in many cases rail emerged as the safer and more reliable travel option, even though the national press made much of the impact of the arctic weather on APT's performance during its first week of public service. That same week also marked the tragic Seer Green accident which occurred in blizzard conditions on 11 December with the loss of four lives—BR's first accident involving passenger fatalities for over two years.

A more wintry prospect is presented at Newport on 11 December when class 47/4 No 47479 drew away with a snow covered Crewe-Cardiff Central service. *(Derek Short)*

Although officially withdrawn, a number of class 306 emus were returned to traffic in December to handle pre-Christmas mail on the GE line. Here a 6-car formation braves the first of the winter's snow at Romford on 9 December with the 1421 mail from Colchester to Liverpool Street. The leading DTOS vehicle bears the number 084 formed by the use of stickers, indicating a "made up" unit retaining the Motor Open Second of the set from which its identity is taken. *(Keith Grafton)*

Freight traffic developments

The first trainload of 36" gas pipes is pictured being loaded onto BDV wagons at Leith Docks on 23 February 1981. The pipes are coated at Leith and are then railed to various destinations in England. *(Colin Boocock)*

The year 1981 saw a continuation of the traffic in steel coil established late the previous year between BSC's Llanwern plant in South Wales and Smederevo, Yugoslavia. These high capacity telescopic sliding body vehicles operated by the German company VTG are used for this service, which runs via the Harwich-Zeebrugge ferry, through Belgium and on to Regensburg in southern Germany, where the steel is transferred to barge for the rest of its journey to Yugoslavia. *(BR)*

As work progressed during 1981 on the Thames Barrier flood prevention project, the rail-borne flow of large stone blocks from Caldon Low, Staffordshire, to Angerstein Wharf came to an end. Here one of the final examples of this unusual traffic leaves the cross-London line at Factory Junction in the care of a class 33 locomotive. *(Brian Garvin)*

The facilities of Freightliners are not restricted to scheduled services. A special movement took place at Reading on 8 September when 44 containers totalling nearly seven hundred tonnes of traffic began to be moved by rail to Liverpool for shipment to a new power station in the Marshall Islands in the Pacific. This forwarding operation was organised by Transtec International Freight Services from their own Cargo Centre sidings in Berkeley Avenue, Reading, on behalf of the British contractors involved. The pictures show a general view of the Cargo Centre sidings before loading commenced and class 47/0 No 47201 about to depart with the loaded Freightliner train. *(Transtec International Freight Services)*

A long familiar sight in Devon and Cornwall now drawing to a close is illustrated in this picture of class 45/1 No 45107 ascending Dainton Bank with freight in July 1981. The rear of the train consists of empty short wheelbase china clay vehicles returning to St Blazey. Under an agreement concluded in 1981 between EEC International and Tiger Railcar Leasing, these outmoded wooden-bodied wagons are soon to be replaced by a fleet of 25 modern air-braked hoppers. This development, together with improved handling facilities both in the West Country and the Potteries, ensures the future of this valuable traffic. *(Roger Penny)*

In the West Country, BR's growing Speedlink network extends to Plymouth Friary and Truro. Here class 45/0 No 45015 heads an up service through the middle road at Totnes station in July 1981. *(Roger Penny)*

29 July 1981

The SR put on an exemplary show on 29 July 1981 for the Royal Wedding of the Prince and Princess of Wales when the celebrated honeymoon special ran from Waterloo to Romsey. Many enthusiasts had hoped the SR might repeat a spectacle which would have added the ultimate cherry to this glittering cake by using preserved 4-6-0 No 850 *Lord Nelson*. This locomotive is, of course, approved for running on BR and hauled the Queen's honeymoon train on the same route. Nevertheless it was the present day pride of Stewarts Lane depot, the beautifully groomed class 73 No 73142 *Broadlands* which officiated. The three-coach train consisted of Mk 2 FK No S13401, Mk 1 BCK No S21268 and the SR General Manager's saloon, No TDB975025. BR excels on such occasions and the efforts the SR put into making the Royal journey such a success on 29 July was a great credit on all staff involved.

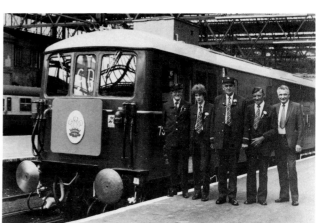

The empty stock was worked into Waterloo from Stewarts Lane by No 73101 *Brighton Evening Argus* and No 73142 *Broadlands*, one locomotive at each end. It is seen here passing Clapham Junction in preparation for the Royal journey. *(Keith Grafton)*

The crew pose next to No 73142 at Waterloo station. From left to right, Driver Bill Turner, Assistant Driver Paul Stoneman, Guard Bill 'Sailor' Simpson, Divisional Motive Power Inspector Cyril Stevens and Divisional Motive Power Officer Bill Neale. *(BR Waterloo)*

With poses of "The Happy Couple" in each window of the engine compartment of their Eastleigh-based class 33 No 33016, a loyal crew await the passage of the Prince and Princess of Wales at Clapham Junction on 29 July 1981. *(Brian Garvin)*

The honeymoon special diverges from the Bournemouth main line at Redbridge as it conveys the Royal couple to Romsey. *(John Chalcraft)*

Running on diesel power, class 73/1 No 73142 *Broadlands* leaves London's Waterloo station for Romsey with the now legendary special train conveying the Prince and Princess of Wales. *(BR SR)*

Several railways in the private sector celebrated the Royal Wedding on 29 July 1981. The North Yorkshire Moors Railway has on loan from the National Railway Museum a headboard formerly carried on Queen Victoria's Royal trains. Suitably adorned, 2-6-4T No 80135 poses at Pickering after arrival from Grosmont. *(Murray Brown)*

Steamtown Carnforth also celebrated the Royal Wedding with this colourful headboard carried by No 850 *Lord Nelson* whilst hauling "The Cumbrian Mountain Express" on 29 July. *(Jim Coleman)*

Continental traffic

In 1981, a new contract was signed for the conveyance of china clay from Cornwall to Switzerland in high capacity Polybulk wagons. In this view, the return empty train of 22 vehicles is seen passing Orpington on 22 June 1981. Loaded wagons are sent forward from St. Blazey as two 11-vehicle trains to Dover. Here each train is split into five- or six-wagon rakes and ferried to Dunkerque where all 22 vehicles are re-formed into one special working for the final stage of the trip to Switzerland. *(Brian Garvin)*

A visit to England by the then newly elected French President M Mitterand provoked a new wave of *entente cordiale* and resulted in a renewed commitment by the governments of both countries to a Channel Tunnel. Meanwhile, BR soldiers on with train ferries for its booming continental traffic. Typical aspects of this activity in 1981 are presented by these views taken on 2 August showing Dover Town Yard, with empty Polybulk vehicles for St Blazey evident behind two stabled class 73s and of Dover Ferry Siding, where two class 09s have just unloaded the *St Eloi* and are preparing to propel onto the vessel its return load. To the left is the Customs inspection shed. (Both: *Brian Garvin*)

Test trains

In poor weather conditions on 10 March 1981, class 50s Nos 50013 and 50002 need all their 5400hp to propel a train of 60 loaded Foster Yeoman Procor hoppers out of Merehead Quarry to gain the former Cheddar Valley line. The purpose of the working was to test the strength of the Procor buffers when under full compression in conjunction with the proposed running of 3000 tonne trains to Yeoman's new aggregates terminal at Theale, Berks. *(John Chalcraft)*

A very significant trial took place in the summer of 1981 which could have a considerable impact on BR's constant efforts to improve customer service and reduce operating costs. An experiment was conducted using a class 25 locomotive, 6 vacuum braked Mk 1 coaches and an airbraked wagon to establish if the formation could operate with both braking systems in operation at the same time. The test followed discussions between Scottish Region and a potential customer seeking an overnight service from Aberdeen to Thurso for delivery to the Orkneys. For the test, special instructions were issued to disregard normal General Appendix operating instructions. A 60ft Freightliner vehicle loaded to 54 tonnes was modified by having a steam pipe fitted beneath it alongside the standard air and vacuum pipes and the rear end of the air pipe was plugged. The test run included nine emergency stops and was conducted at speeds varying between 20 and 75mph. One of its purposes was to ascertain if the faster operating air brake produced unacceptable jolting for passengers in the vacuum-braked stock, but sensoring equipment revealed that this was not a problem. The test run commenced at Motherwell with class 25/2 No 25233 in charge. It is pictured during this unique and successful experiment near Shotts. *(BR Glasgow)*

Doubtful future?

During 1981 BR announced that it was to re-route the through passenger trains presently using the Settle and Carlisle line via Manchester and the West Coast main line. This news added further pointers to the line's possible closure as a through route, especially in view of the spiralling cost of maintaining Ribblehead viaduct. Principal services affected by such a move would be the Nottingham-Glasgow trains. In this view class 47/4 No 47524 leaves Skipton with the 0715 Nottingham-Glasgow on 11 September 1981. *(John Chalcraft)*

Class 87 No 87023 *Highland Chieftain* passes Basford Hall Junction on 12 September 1981 with the 0905SO Perth-Kensington Olympia Motorail service. The recession has affected Motorail business and one of the economies planned for 1982 was to close Kensington as a Motorail terminus, transfer the traffic to Euston and Paddington and run the carflats separately, with vehicle owners travelling by scheduled passenger services. *(Barry Nicolle)*

Diesel specials continued in earnest in 1981 proving yet again that steam is not the only attraction. Tours covered many parts of the country and BR were co-operative in providing where possible unusual motive power on several specials. However, the year also saw some specials cancelled due to lack of motive power and the sharp rise in prices together with the diminishing sets of Mk 1 stock was an omen that in 1982 the trend may be towards fewer specials than hitherto. A selection of several of the year's railtours is featured here. Others will be found in our Deltic feature at the front of the book.

Winter in spring! In unseasonal conditions on 26 April 1981, class 47/0 No 47033 draws to a stand at Gloucester with the NREA 'South Wales Double' railtour. Due to severe snow in the Cotswolds, the train formed the first service train over the Swindon-Gloucester route that morning, being used by BR to convey fare paying passengers. *(John Chalcraft)*

Diesel-hauled railtours

On 18 April 1981 Hertfordshire Railtours organised the 'Shoulder of Lune' tour which embraced a circular tour from Euston to Heysham. The setting is Edale where class 40 No 40120 is heading east for Sheffield. *(Les Nixon)*

On 14 June 1981 a locomotive hauled passenger train reached Harwich Town in the form of class 37 No 37023 hauling the F & W Railtours 'Anglian Adventurer'. The train is seen awaiting departure for the west. (John Chalcraft)

The 'Doncaster Dart' tour on 26 July 1981 is pictured at Mexborough during a photo stop. Laira depot, Plymouth had provided as train engine class 50 No 50025 Invincible (in old livery) but had used the working to return No 50040 Leviathan to Doncaster Works for rectification work. (Norman Preedy)

A three-day tour also run by F & W Railtours visited Stranraer, Perth, Forfar, Aberdeen, Edinburgh, Carlisle and Newcastle. The tour reached Stranraer on 18 September with class 40 No 40024. Class 27 No 27012 officiated by releasing the class 40 from the bufferstops. Passengers on this tour, titled 'The Ayr Aberdonian', had the choice of riding behind No 27012 or photographing it removing the stock. (John Chalcraft)

The following day the tour visited the threatened freight only branch from Perth to Forfar, following the route of the former main line from Perth to Aberdeen via Forfar and Brechin. The line beyond Forfar to Kinnaber Junction was closed as a through route from 4 September 1967. Class 37 No 37026 was in charge of the railtour when photographed at Forfar station on 19 September 1981. (John Chalcraft)

Class 20s are frequently requested for railtours in view of their infrequent use on passenger trains. On 4 October 1981, Nos 20178 and 20148 worked the NREA 'Doncaster Double' railtour which was pictured at Derby. Due to engineering works, the tour was routed outwards via Derby (with reversal) and Toton Yard to gain the Erewash Valley route to the north. (*John Chalcraft*)

F & W Railtours ran 'The Yorkshire Greyhound' on 10 October 1981 with a destination of Whitby. From Stockport to York passengers had to endure non-boilered class 40 No 40182 before it was replaced by two class 31s for the run to Whitby. A cold photographer captures the moment in the early hours on platform 14 at York. (*John Chalcraft*)

A class 50 returned to its old haunts on 31 October 1981 when No 50011 *Centurion* headed for Carlisle from Plymouth with 'The Citadel Express' organised by Severnside Railtours. The class 50 poses for the cameras during a photo stop at Horton-in-Ribblesdale. (*John Chalcraft*)

PRESERVATION

Open for business

Several railways opened their doors to the public in 1981. These included the Midland Railway Trust at Butterley, the Bo'ness Railway operated by the SRPS and the Llangollen Railway, featured on p 2. In this view class 4F 0-6-0 No 4027 departs from Butterley on 29 August 1981, passing 'Jinty' No 16440 *(Tom Heavyside)*

Despite the many prophets of doom who have for some years been predicting that the preservation bubble is about to burst, no sign of that was evident in 1981, although the recession took its toll and several private railways sustained a drop in revenue.

Steam is very much alive with several locomotives making their debut during the year after restoration and other old favourites making their comeback after major overhaul. One surprising aspect of 1981 was the growing number of privately preserved diesel locomotives—a sign of the times—and while some established 'diesel' lines increased their allocations, others previously all steam worked succumbed after previously refusing to entertain this mode of traction.

On 27 June 1981 the Bo'ness Railway welcomed the public. An ambitious programme is well under way here to provide an extensive system for steam lovers. 0-6-0T No 24, a former tenant of the magnificent Waterside NCB system at Ayr, is pictured at the new station at Bo'ness. The station building originates from Wormit, at the south end of the Tay Bridge. *(Stuart Sellar)*

Steam
in Bristol

The River Avon had steam drifting over its waters in July 1981. The reproduction *Rocket* was on display at the Bristol Industrial Museum in conjunction with the presentation of the World Wine Fair. (*John Chalcraft*)

For three weeks in October 1981, live steam returned to the centre of Bristol when the Bristol Industrial Museum's Peckett 0-6-0ST *Henbury* was hired to the neighbouring Western Fuel Company during the absence of their 0-6-0 diesel shunter. *Henbury* was photographed on the quayside enjoying the unexpected limelight. (*John Chalcraft*)

Steamed again

For the first time since 1938, Stirling Single No 1 raised steam at the rear of the NRM's Annexe on 18 June 1981. In view of its age, the NRM considered it prudent to lower the boiler pressure to 110psi. The GNR veteran was later loaned to the Great Central Railway at Loughborough, where it worked certain services on 5 and 6 December. *(John Bellwood)*

The Bluebell Railway was the scene on 13 June 1981 of the official return to steam of 'Schools' 4-4-0 No 928 *Stowe*. To mark the occasion Lord Montagu unveiled one nameplate whilst Mr S C Townroe former Shedmaster at Bournemouth, final BR home of *Stowe*, unveiled the other. The locomotive was first lit on 5 June after 18 years inactivity. It was obtained in 1963 by Lord Montagu for display at Beaulieu together with three Pullman cars, remaining there until expansion of the Montagu (now National) Motor Museum led to both *Stowe* and the Pullmans being found new homes. No 928 moved to the East Somerset Railway before going to the Bluebell for restoration to working order. She is pictured here near Sheffield Park on a running in turn on 8 June 1981. *(Roger Cruse)*

Llywelyn *in green livery*

Highlights of the 1981 season on BR's Vale of Rheidol line were the reappearance of No 8 *Llywelyn* in GWR green and the decision to name the early afternoon return trip from Aberstwyth 'The Welsh Dragon'. Here, appropriately headboarded, No 8 leads the 1415 from Aberystwyth round the final curve into Devil's Bridge on 11 May, just one week after introduction of the named service. *(L Collin)*

7F *in action*

Memories of the legendary Somerset & Dorset Joint Railway were relived on 2 May 1981 when class 7F No 13809 had its first main line run up the Hope Valley and on to York. The 2-8-0 is seen in full cry at Chinley hauling 'The Pines Express'. *(Jim Coleman)*

Compound interest

Midland Compound No 1000 had a day out on the 'Yorkshire Circular' route on 7 October when it hauled a three-coach special train consisting of the two Metro-Cammell Pullmans and the LNWR Brake. The train was run to mark a contract signing between wagon manufacturer Procor and the Ford Motor Company. The locomotive presents a beautiful sight as the train passes under the A59 York to Harrogate road, just west of Poppleton. *(Peter Skelton)*

Earlier in the year on 1 July, the Compound, together with a three-coach rake of LMS carriages, was used as a prop during the filming of an Ovaltine advertisement at York station. Carriages used were LMS period 1 SLT No 14241, period 1 TO No KDM 395345 and period 111 BTK No M27093M, the last two being from the former LMR mobile control train acquired by the NRM. The filming provided for passing travellers the interesting spectacle of children being evacuated complete with cloth caps and gas masks! No 1000 made several starts from the bay, delighting photographers standing on adjacent platform 8S. *(Stephen Bellamy)*

Distant A4s

The ever popular No 60009 *Union of South Africa* delighted A4 fans on several occasions during 1981. One of these outings took place on 18 April 1981 when the locomotive was pictured skirting the River Tay near Invergowrie. *(Colin Sykes)*

No 4498 *Sir Nigel Gresley* was also used extensively in 1981 and this view of the A4 in charge of 'The Lancastrian' crossing Whalley Arches on 23 May 1981 highlights the increased use made of the Hellifield-Blackburn route for steam specials during the year. *(Jim Coleman)*

Steam returned to Stewarts Lane depot, London on the Southern Region for the first time in possibly 15 years when on 16 May 1981 0-6-0ST 'Austerity' No 23 *Holman F Stephens* arrived by road transporter from the Kent & East Sussex Railway for tyre turning. It was thought more convenient to move the tank complete by road for this operation than to remove the wheelsets from the locomotive. No 23 stayed for one week at the depot and was shunted on arrival by class 73/1 No 73112. *(M Vine)*

KESR events

The KESR's 'Steam & Country Fair' is now an established part of the Kentish calendar and last year's event took place on 19 September 1981, when the two main attractions were undoubtedly the replica *Rocket* and 0-6-0T 'Terrier' *Fenchurch*. The latter locomotive had been loaned by the Bluebell Railway and proceeds from the event were to be put towards restoration of the KESR's own 'Terrier', *Stepney*. Both locomotives parade past Tenterden Town station on 19 September 1981. *(Brian Cooke)*

Following its remarkable steaming at York in June (see page 101), GNR Stirling Single No 1 was sent to the Great Central Railway at Loughborough, where it staged a memorable series of runs on 5 and 6 December. The 4-2-2 made this dramatic departure from Loughborough's distinctive station with its first passenger carrying train in over 40 years. *(Brian Cooke)*

Class 4 2-6-4T No 80064 returned to steam in 1981 on the Dart Valley Railway. It was built at Brighton in 1953 and saw service during its active career in the London area of the LMR followed by a stay on the SR. Its final home was on the WR and it was withdrawn from service in 1965 from Bristol Barrow Road. No 80064 was rescued from Barry scrapyard by the members of the 80064 Locomotive Group and arrived at Buckfastleigh on the Dart Valley Railway on 2 February 1973 after a journey by road lasting over one week. Eight years of painstaking restoration by volunteer labour then followed and No 80064 was steamed for the first time on 23 February 1981. After running in, it is hoped that the locomotive will be available for traffic for the 1982 season. *(Roger Penny)*

Back in steam

The Kent & East Sussex Railway returned USA 0-6-0T No 22 *Maunsell* to steam in 1981. Attending the ceremony to mark the tank's re-entry into service were US naval personnel from the visiting *USS Claude V Ricketts* at Portsmouth. The date was 4 April 1981. *(Jim Berryman)*

On 24 April, the Mid Hants' U class 2-6-0 No 31806 was lit for the first time since salvation from Barry scrapyard. This much admired locomotive was photographed hauling the 1725 Alresford-Ropley train on 23 August 1981. The SR 4-wheeled PMV and the inclusion by the photographer of the SR pw hut add further authenticity to the scene. *(Tom Heavyside)*

On 21 June 1981, 'Terrier' No W8 *Freshwater* was returned to traffic on the Isle of Wight Steam Railway. The locomotive was built by the London Brighton & South Coast Railway as No 46; in 1903 it was sold to the London & South Western Railway who loaned (and later sold) the locomotive to the Freshwater, Yarmouth & Newport Railway. It passed into Southern Railway hands becoming No W2, was named *Freshwater* and subsequently renumbered W8. In 1949 it was returned by British Railways to the mainland to serve out its days on the Hayling Island branch. Initially privately preserved at Droxford, it was sold to Brickwoods to be a novel "sign" outside their *Hayling Billy* public house. Whitbreads, successors to Brickwoods, kindly donated the locomotive to the Wight Locomotive Society in 1979.

After speeches (in this view we see Society Chairman, Roger Silsbury, accompanied by Vice President, Sir Peter Allen) *Freshwater* hauled a special train between Haven Street and Wootton for invited guests and Society members before working most of the remainder of the day's scheduled services. *(Isle of Wight Steam Railway)*

Class 9F No 92220 *Evening Star* was overhauled by the GWS at Didcot and steamed again in September 1981. The 9F is seen on the demonstration line at Didcot on 26 September 1981. *(Tom Heavyside)*

The Great Western Society's auto train consisting of 0-4-2T No 1466 and auto coach No W231W returned to the public's admiration at Didcot on 15 August 1981. This view was taken on 26 September. *(Tom Heavyside)*

Friday the 13th is lucky for some! This was the day in February when BR 4-6-0 No 75014 was unloaded at its new home, the North Yorkshire Moors Railway. The Standard class 4MT is owned by the 75014 Locomotive Operators Group, a consortium of four NYMR members. A tender of the correct type for this class had previously been purchased and No 75014 was later towed to Grosmont for restoration. It is photographed at New Bridge, Pickering preparatory to unloading. *(Brian Cooke)*

The Barry saga

The year 1981 was a busy one at Mr Dai Woodham's Barry scrapyard, witnessing increasing interest as the numbers of locomotives dwindled or were reserved. In addition the recommencement of scrapping, albeit temporary, rekindled and gave fresh impetus to existing and new schemes. Inaugurated in February, the 'Barry Rescue' operation, in which Mr Robert Adley MP was prominent, became incorporated into the National Railway Preservation Campaign. The year also saw completion of the widely publicised locomotive survey at Barry yard conducted by Mr John Peck and Mr George Knight,

both of whom had recently retired from BR at Leeds and Derby respectively. The recession may have been responsible for the lack of funds optimistically anticipated from industry, but this was counterbalanced by the completion of fund raising, reservations, and new purchases which, by the end of the year, had reduced the number of unreserved locomotives to under 20. This figure was an indication of the unceasing demand for Barry locomotives, aided without doubt by Mr Woodham and the Barry Steam Locomotive Action Group. We are indebted to the latter organisation for the following information.

Departures from Barry yard during 1981 included:

JANUARY
SR 4-6-2 No 34067 *Tangmere*
  Mid Hants Railway

FEBRUARY
GWR 0-6-0PT No 4612
  Keighley & Worth Valley Railway
GWR 2-6-2T No 4121
  Dean Forest Railway (for spare parts)
BR 4-6-0 No 75014
  North Yorkshire Moors Railway

MARCH
SR 4-6-0 No 30828
  Eastleigh Railway Preservation Society
GWR 2-8-0 No 2885
  GWR Preservation Group, Southall

APRIL
GWR 2-6-2T No 5532
  Dean Forest Railway (for spare parts)

MAY
GWR 4-6-0 No 5972 *Olton Hall*
  Privately purchased, c/o Procor Ltd,
  Wakefield
GWR 4-6-0 No 4936 *Kinlet Hall*
  Peak Railway
SR 4-6-2 No 34007 *Wadebridge*
  Plym Valley Railway Association
GWR 0-6-0PT No 9629
  Commonwealth Holiday Inns Ltd (to be
  restored at Carnforth as static exhibit for
  display in new Cardiff Holiday Inn)

JUNE
GWR 4-6-0 No 7903 *Foremarke Hall*
  Swindon & Cricklade Railway
GWR 2-8-0 No 2807
  Gloucestershire & Warwickshire Railway
GWR 0-6-2T No 6634
  East Somerset Railway
GWR 4-6-0 No 7821 *Ditcheat Manor*

Gloucestershire & Warwickshire Railway
GWR 4-6-0 No 7828 *Odney Manor*
  Gloucestershire & Warwickshire Railway

JULY
LMS 4-6-0 No 45491
  West Lancs Black Five Fund c/o ICI Ltd,
  Fleetwood

LMS 2-8-0 No 48624
  Peak Railway

SEPTEMBER
GWR 4-6-0 No 5952 *Cogan Hall*
  Gloucestershire & Warwickshire Railway
GWR 2-8-2T No 7200
  Quainton Railway Centre

The last entry was the 137th departure from Barry. The 1981 removals are listed not with the actual purchasers but with the location where the individual locomotives are to be restored or displayed.

GWR Class 6959 4-6-0 No 7903 *Foremarke Hall* has returned to its birthplace—well nearly so! The Foremarke Hall Locomotive Ltd purchased No 7903 for the Swindon & Cricklade Railway, its first Barry locomotive. The 'Modified Hall' made a guest appearance at the BREL Swindon Open Day on 6 June before proceeding to its new home at Blunsdon the following day. It is seen awaiting an assured future at Blunsdon shortly after arrival. *(Pete Nicholson)*

The first locomotive to be delivered to the Toddington site of the Gloucestershire & Warwickshire Railway was ex-GWR 2-8-0 No 2807. Built in 1905, this locomotive had the distinction of being the oldest in Barry yard and was purchased on 12 March by the Cotswold Steam Preservation Company supported by the Churchward 'Consolidation' Fund. No 2807 left Barry on 19 June 1981 and was pictured the following morning in a lay-by on the Newport to Monmouth road. *(Pete Nicholson)*

The Peak Railway, which plans eventually to re-open the former Midland main line from Matlock to Buxton, made significant progress in 1981 by securing locomotives and, more importantly, planning permission from the various authorities through whose areas the line passes. Class 8F No 48624 is one of the future fleet of Peak Rail Operations and was moved from Barry scrapyard on 31 July 1981. It is pictured at Buxton with class 9F No 92214 in the background. The date was 5 September 1981. *(John Chalcraft)*

The only complete and operational AC Cars railbus, formerly BR No W79978, was purchased from the North Yorkshire Moors Railway in 1981 by the Kent & East Sussex Railway. At its new home, the railbus is seen at Dixter Halt. Although regular steam and diesel trains run only between Tenterden and Wittersham at present, the line will be extended to Bodiam in due course. Dixter Halt, opened in 1981 to serve the nearby Great Dixter Hall, is on this closed section but on certain Bank Holidays and summer Sundays, the railbus operates between the halt and Bodiam, a distance of 2 miles. *(Brian Stephenson)*

Open
and shut

Newtondale Halt on the North Yorkshire Moors Railway was officially opened on 15 June 1981 by Mr Hector Monro, MP, Parliamentary Under Secretary of State for the Environment. The new halt has been provided for walkers in the heart of Newtondale and three waymarked walks have been designated. With considerable involvement by Forestry Commission, the halt was built from the remains of Warrenby station on Teesside. It is believed that Newtondale Halt has the distinction of being the British station most distant from a highway—that is, unless any reader knows differently. *(Yorkshire Post)*

The Derwent Valley Railway closed its 4½ mile line from Layerthorpe, York, to Dunnington on 27 September 1981. The line's economic situation had worsened when its main traffic of malting barley was hit by falling whisky sales. A final farewell trip was organised by the BR Eastern Region Staff Railway Society using five coaches hired from BR. The DVR's *The Lord Wenlock* (ex-BR No D2298), driven by Ken Bell, was used for the last train which is pictured approaching York after passing under the city by-pass. The DVR will still be in being as the company has other interests and a small section of line will be retained at Murton as an agricultural museum. *(Stephen Bellamy)*

Twenty-one years is a grand old age in the private railway sector and the Talyllyn Railway achieved this commendable distinction in 1981. A festive weekend was held on 2 and 3 May and two of the highlights are shown here. TRPS President and Railway Company Chairman Pat Garland unveils the replica maker's plate on No 4 *Edward Thomas* at Wharf station on 2 May (the locomotive's "official" 60th birthday) assisted by Railway Company Managing Director and TRPS Council member Bill Faulkner, who is also a volunteer driver. *(David Mitchell)*

On the narrow gauge

And they said that they would never do it! Five locomotives in steam at Wharf station. From the front: No 4 *Edward Thomas*, No 3 *Sir Haydn*, No 1 *Talyllyn*, No 2 *Dolgoch* and No 6 *Douglas*. This line-up was photographed on 2 May 1981. *(John Slater)*

The Brecon Mountain Railway, one of the newest of 'The Great Little Trains of Wales', saw the return to steam in 1981 of Jung-built (1908) No 1261 *Graf Schwerin-Löwitz*. This handsome new addition to the fleet is pictured at Pontsticill on 30 June 1981. *(Tom Heavyside)*

On 18 July 1981, after a gap of 21 years, the Welshpool & Llanfair Railway once again operated into Welshpool, where a new station at Raven Square has been built. The 2¾ mile Sylfaen-Welshpool formation, which includes the 1 in 30 Golfa incline, took four years to complete at a cost of over £70,000. Locomotive No 10 *Sir Drefaldwyn*, an 0-8-0T built by Franco-Belge in 1944, hauled the first train into Raven Square, where it was met by the Mayor and Mayoress of Welshpool. After speeches, the Mayor flagged away the train at 1230. The picture shows former Sierra Leone Railways 2-6-2T No 14 with ex-Zillertalbahn and West African coaching stock in the new station shortly after opening. The newly repainted Upnor van No 213 on the right was serving as a temporary ticket office. *(Ralph Cartwright)*

Diesels preserved

The Bury Transport Museum and the associated East Lancashire Railway clearly encourages hydraulic traction for class 42 No D832 *Onslaught* and class 52 No D1041 *Western Lady* have been given a home at this interesting venue. Peeping out of the new shed on 29 March 1981 was No D832 whilst No D1041 was tucked up inside. *(Tom Heavyside)*

It was a good year for hydraulics on the North Yorkshire Moors Railway. At Easter, the Diesel Traction Group's class 35 'Hymek' No D7029 and class 42 'Warship' No D821 *Greyhound* arrived from Swindon Works where they had resided for eight years. Both diesels have become considerable attractions and, due to the poor availability of steam traction, each ran over 1000 miles during the season.

The Moors Railway also purchased two class 14 'Teddybear' locomotives from BSC, Corby. These were formerly BR Nos D9520 and D9529 and original liveries are planned for both machines. Both are pictured on Grosmont shed shortly after arrival. Other examples of this type during 1981 found homes on the Great Central Railway, the Scottish RPS at Falkirk and on the West Somerset Railway. *(Michael McMurray)*

One of the last class 24 survivors was purchased for preservation in 1981. This is No 24081 and it can be seen at the Southport Transport Museum, where it was photographed on 30 August 1981. *(Tom Heavyside)*

Two of the class 44 'Peaks' have survived for future generations. No 44004 formerly *Great Gable* now has a home on the Midland Railway Trust at Butterley and No 44008, formerly *Penyghent*, has found new status at Aviemore on the Strathspey Railway. It was one of the exhibits at the Glasgow Works Open Day on 27 June 1981 whilst en route to Aviemore. *(Keith Grafton)*

The NRM's class 52 No D1023 *Western Fusilier* arrived at Paignton on the Dart Valley Railway's Torbay line on 8 July for a two year period. After receiving an overhaul at BREL Swindon, the locomotive went into service on the mid-week evening "Sundowner" excursions and on Saturday trains. In this picture No D1023 is crossing Broadsands viaduct on a dull September afternoon. *(Roger Penny)*

Mid Hants looks ahead

Looking towards Alton.

In 1981 the Mid Hants Railway was actively planning re-instatement of its line to connect with BR at Alton. The way ahead (and back) at Medstead on 4 October shows the magnitude of the task.

Looking towards Ropley. (All: *Brian Cooke*)

NOTICE

THIS LAND AND BUILDINGS ARE OWNED BY THE WINCHESTER AND ALTON RAILWAY LIMITED. IT IS HOPED TO REINTRODUCE A RAIL SERVICE IN THE NEAR FUTURE. YOU ARE REQUESTED NOT TO CAUSE DAMAGE AS THIS MAY DELAY THE REOPENING. ANYONE INTERESTED IN VOLUNTEER WORK ON THIS SITE CONTACT INFORMATION OFFICE, ALRESFORD STATION.

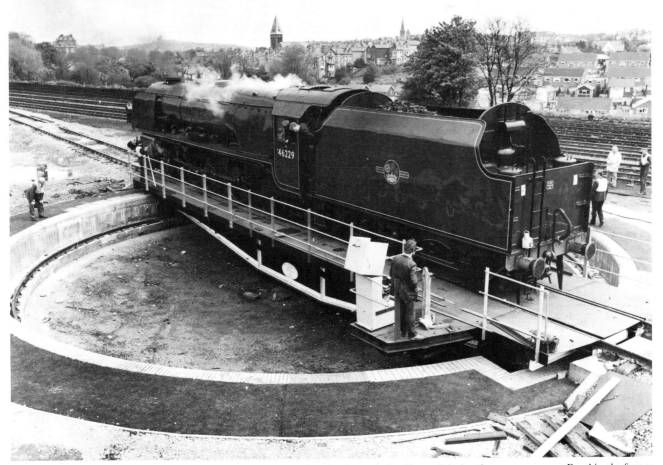

BR Eastern Region returned to the steam scene in 1981, running 'The Scarborough Spa Express' during the summer season. For this, the former Gateshead 60ft turntable was installed in the pit of the old Scarborough turntable. To accommodate the largest locomotives to be used on the service, it was necessary to lengthen the table by 10ft and this was accomplished by adding 5ft sections at both ends. The original 60ft well was retained with the table being raised so that the lengthened ends overhung the well wall. Tests were carried out with a class 40 diesel and considerable difficulty was experienced in aligning the table. Just prior to the commencement of the steam service, No 46229 *Duchess of Hamilton* was sent to Scarborough for a final trial of the turntable. *(BR ER)*

The tables are turned

Churston turntable on the Torbay line of the Dart Valley Railway Company became operational during last year. It was manufactured by Ransomes and Rapier and installed at Goodrington in 1955 as part of the additional facilities provided there at that time. Acquired by the Dart Valley Railway in 1976, it was subsequently moved to Churston where restoration and installation took place. The culmination of five years hard work, including the manufacture of many missing parts, came to fruition when the 65ft long 149 ton capacity turntable was used for the first time in April 1981. 2-8-0T No 5239 *Goliath* was the first locomotive to be turned, on 16 April. *(Roger Penny)*

Didcot visitors

The superbly nicknamed 'Flying Pig' 2-6-0 No 43106 ventured forth onto BR lines with a special named after it on 11 April 1981. Didcot was its southern destination where the locomotive is seen taking on coal during preparations at the Great Western Society's depot for its return journey to Birmingham. *(Ken Harris)*

Celebrated Liverpool & Manchester Railway veteran *Lion* toured several railway centres during 1981 including Tyseley, Dinting, the Keighley & Worth Valley and Didcot. It was pictured at this latter location on 26 September 1981. *(Tom Heavyside)*

Society events

This picture could have been taken decades ago but in reality was taken on 12 September 1981 and shows class 57XX 0-6-0PT No 5764 heading through Bewdley with a short freight, one of the many attractions of the Enthusiasts' Weekend. *(Dave Walden)*

The Severn Valley Railway offers one of the finest Enthusiasts' Weekend in terms of the number of locomotives in action and the 1981 event on 12 and 13 September was very popular. The notice board at Hampton Loade for the Sunday's workings was impressive with even D1013 *Western Ranger* in steam—for heating the carriages of course! *(Brian Cooke)*

Guest of honour of the Dean Forest Railway Society at Norchard on the August Bank Holiday open day was the Rev Wilbert Awdry, author of the well known childrens' railway books. A life member of the Society, he had consented to name Hunslet 'Austerity' 0-6-0ST No 3806, which was built at Leeds in 1953. The name *G. B. Keeling* was chosen by DFR members from a shortlist of five names closely associated with the Severn & Wye Railway, the only remaining section of which exists between Lydney and Parkend. No 3806 was purchased by a group of society members in 1972. Restoration commenced after the tank passed into society ownership in 1975 and was completed in 1981. The Rev Awdry here enjoys a footplate ride following the naming ceremony on 31 August 1981. *(Peter Skelton)*

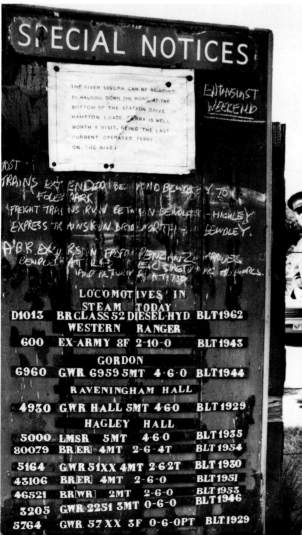

Industrial retirements

Agecroft power station, one of the last strongholds of industrial steam in the north-west finally succumbed on 12 September with a 'Farewell To Steam Day'. *Agecroft No 3*, an 0-4-0ST built by Robert Stephenson Hawthorn in 1951 entertained visitors and mourners in two replica Liverpool & Manchester Railway coaches. *(Tom Heavyside)*

This 0-4-0ST, *Birkenhead*, had the distinction of being the last working steam locomotive in London when, with *Little Barford*, it brought to an end steam operation at Acton Lane Power Station on 28 February 1981. Luckily, *Birkenhead* built in 1948 by Robert Stephenson & Hawthorn No 7386, can still be seen working in the London vicinity as it has found a new home at the Great Western Railway Preservation Group's depot at Southall, at which location it was pictured on 27 September 1981. *(Tom Heavyside)*

Two anniversaries

The Middleton Railway at Leeds celebrated its 21st Anniversary on 5 September and freight trains were one of the main attractions of the day. The Middleton Railway is one private line which handles freight traffic as part of its daily routine, incoming scrap being the commodity handled. On the celebration day for which, incidently, BR Leeds provided a 'Railfreight' wagon, 0-4-0ST No P2003 moves the special freight between BR's exchange sidings and Tunstall Road Halt. *(Tom Heavyside)*

No W24 *Calbourne* entered service 90 years ago as London & South Western Railway No 209. To mark this anniversary a short ceremony was held immediately before the last departure of the Isle of Wight Steam Railway's 1981 season. Two bricket cakes were "fed" into *Calbourne's* firebox, whilst the volunteer workforce shared two rather more conventional birthday cakes! *Calbourne* is seen here departing Haven Street immediately after these jollifications with the 1645 to Wootton on Sunday 27 September. *(Isle of Wight Steam Railway)*

A privately owned 1907-built GNR saloon which used to reside at Carnforth began a new career in the spring of 1981 at Jesmond, Newcastle. The saloon, No 397, was bought by three Newcastle businessmen and has now become part of 'The Carriage', an up-market hostelry which opened its doors to the public on 1 April 1981. 'The Carriage' is housed in what used to be Jesmond Road station in the well populated inner suburb of Jesmond, about a mile from Newcastle city centre. Since preservation No 397 was certificated to run on BR and hauled by No 4472 *Flying Scotsman* visited Doncaster 'Railex 125' exhibition in 1977. The vehicle is pictured soon after opening to the public in April 1981. *(Peter Robinson)*

A unique catering vehicle, BAR coach No E1883, was sold for preservation in 1981. The coach was built in 1968 by Chas Roberts and ended its working days in a Newcastle-Cardiff set. On withdrawal at York, the vehicle was initially sold for scrap but the Stour Valley Railway stepped in to save it. Now residing at Chappel and Wakes Colne where it was delivered by road from York (the bogies were returned to BR under the conditions of sale), the coach presently rests on two piles of sleepers. *(Chris Wright)*

Rolling stock developments

Three magnificent Gresley coaches from the former Eastern Region mobile control trains found a new home on the Yorkshire Dales Railway at Embsay in 1981. The vehicles, open thirds to diagram 186, are numbered TDE321001, TDE321002 and TDE321006 and were all built in 1935. They were bought privately at Doncaster Carr depot and had formed part of the four 4-coach mobile control trains allocated to the Eastern Region. Condemned on 3 August 1979, they had remained at Doncaster until the connection had been installed at Embsay Junction linking the YDR and BR. The coaches were in sound condition having been kept under cover for many years and, after fitting with chairs, were soon in revenue service. They are seen at Embsay on a wet Sunday in May 1981. *(Murray Brown)*

The National Railway Museum has claimed for its collection this 1910-built ex-GCR diagram 67 'Barnum' coach, which was condemned on 17 August. The vehicle is pictured at Barnetby shortly before withdrawal. *(Murray Brown)*

A remarkable train was unveiled to the press on 10 November 1981 at Victoria station, London. Four beautifully restored Pullmans and a former LNER Bogied Pigeon Brake were on view as part of the British section of a proposed Venice-Simplon-Orient Express which is to commence operation in May 1982. This ambitious scheme has been executed to the highest possible standards and has set out to replace South African Railways' Capetown-Johannesburg 'Blue Train' as the finest in the world. The London Victoria-Folkestone section is to be operated by Pullman cars and twelve such vehicles have been obtained since 1977, when the venture was inaugurated by Sea Container Services Ltd. Altogether a staggering £11m has been invested in this enterprising project and unrivalled attention to restoration has been put into the 35 vehicles obtained for the service. The Pullmans have been completely rebuilt at Carnforth and have been equipped with air conditioning, electric heating and new wiring. An interesting modification was the fitting of LNER heavy duty 'JJ' bogies. Another link with the LNER is the provision of the 'Baggage Car' which was formerly E70741 built in 1942. The vehicles on show at Victoria were First class Kitchen Car *Ibis*, First Class Parlour Cars *Cygnus*, *Perseus* and *Phoenix* together with the Brake which has been given the number 7. The photographs show *Perseus* and *Cygnus* outside the workshop at Carnforth and an interior view of a restored Pullman. *(both Sea Container Services Ltd)*

From foreign parts

The much publicised Chinese Government Railway's 4-8-4 No 607 arrived at Tilbury on 26 June 1981. The tender and locomotive were conveyed separately by road arriving in York on 2 July and 3 July respectively. Following unloading at BREL Carriage Works, the 4-8-4 was moved by rail to the Peter Allen Building (the Annexe) for cosmetic restoration before exhibition. The Friends of the NRM agreed to finance the cost of this renovation. Work included removal of the lagging on the boiler which soaked up sea water and moisture during the five months voyage from Shanghai. The picture shows Phil Atkins, Librarian, NRM, dwarfed by the Vulcan Foundry-built (1935) 4-8-4 after arrival at York on 3 July 1981. *(National Railway Museum)*

Swedish ladies are usually very popular and 4-6-0 No 1313 was no exception in 1981 when Scottish Railway Preservation Society member William Crawford decided to have her to himself! This 4-6-0 had been in store at Morjarv in the north of Sweden and travelled to Britain from Gothenburg to Middlesbrough, being shipped on the roll-on roll-off vessel *Elk*. The Swedish class B locomotive completed its journey to Bo'ness by road arriving on 7 October when the photograph was taken. *(William Crawford)*

STEAM ON BR

The steam scene on BR during 1981 saw several developments to attract the enthusiast and, looking back at BR's initiatives in promoting their own steam services in 1981, it was hard to realise that October saw the tenth anniversary of 'Return to Steam' on BR. 'The Scarborough Spa Express' was the Eastern Region's innovation, replacing the Yorkshire circular route, whilst the North and West route from Shrewsbury to Newport was host to 'The Welsh Marches Express'. Besides such established favourites as 'The Cumbrian Coast Express' and 'The Cumbrian Mountain Express' based at Carnforth, the Leeds to Northwich route via Diggle became a regular itinerary in 1981. Considering the importance of this Trans-Pennine artery, this was confirmation that BR were indeed confident in the abilities of approved locomotives on a main route as opposed to the usual secondary lines.

The ER and LMR also co-operated in operating six Sunday excursions from 26 July with steam traction between York and Carnforth, a popular development which provided passengers with different locomotives for out and home journeys and which also provided a means of supplying York with varying motive power to work 'The Scarborough Spa Express'.

'New' locomotives to the approved list included 7F No 13809, WC 34092 *City of Wells* and class 4 No 43106. A renewed welcome was extended to 9F No 92220 *Evening Star*, K1 No 2005, 'Castle' No 7029 *Clun Castle* and 'Jubilee' No 5690 *Leander*, all of which returned to the main line after absences under repair.

Runpasts at such locations as Abergavenny, Wennington, Clapham and Appleby provided some spectacular photography and were a new regular feature in 1981 much appreciated by tour participants. Not so encouraging were the disappointing loadings on certain specials, perhaps an indication that over-exposure of steam could result in a cut-back in operations. One continuing and surprising feature of 1981, and possibly a contributory factor to poor ticket sales, was the running of more than one steam tour on the same day. In one instance, no less than three steam tours ran simultaneously in the north of England, all competing for custom.

'West Country' Pacific No 34092 *City of Wells*, usually resident on the Keighley and Worth Valley Railway, made a welcome return to main line running in 1981. Complete with 'Golden Arrow' finery and in sub-zero temperatures, she is seen approaching Melling tunnel on the outward run from Carnforth on 12 December. 'City of Wells' is featured again on p136. *(Ted Parker)*

Welsh Marches Express

Stanier Pacific No 6201 *Princess Elizabeth* was a regular performer on the North and West route in 1981. It is seen near the summit at Llanvihangel with the southbound 'Welsh Marches Express' on 25 April, and in an earlier view waiting to take over the same train at Shrewsbury on 7 March. *(Peter Skelton, Ken Harris)*

Ex-GWR 4-6-0 No 4930 *Hagley Hall* made its solo main line debut in 1981 when it became a popular performer on the 'Welsh Marches Express'. Two views are featured of No 4930 on this duty on 14 March 1981 whilst working the Hereford-Newport leg. The 'Hall' is seen in fine form passing Pontrilas and accelerating away from the Abergavenny photo-stop towards Newport. *(Les Nixon, Peter Skelton)*

A novel attraction of the 'Welsh Marches Express' much appreciated by passengers and roving photographers was the inclusion of run-pasts. The National Railway Museum's 'Black Five' No 5000, which is based on the Severn Valley Railway, starts its run-past at Abergavenny on 7 March 1981. *(Tom Heavyside)*

Lord Nelson's travels

The quiet exhaust of 4-cylinder 4-6-0 No 850 *Lord Nelson* belies the concealed power in this popular locomotive which saw extensive use in 1981 on a variety of routes. The grandeur of the Settle & Carlisle is evident as No 850 has Arten Gill in its sights whilst hauling the southbound CME away from Dent on 29 July 1981. On this day the train was named 'The Wedding Belle'. *(Peter Skelton)*

Lord Nelson was a guest of Northwich shed on 20 June 1981 prior to working across to Leeds. North-wich, formerly shed code 8E, has been host to numerous preserved locomotives, coming into prominence in 1981 with the regular Trans-Pennine specials. *(Tom Heavyside)*

A special train was run on 11 March from Liverpool Lime Street to York to commemorate the 150th anniversary of carrying troops by rail. SR No 850 "Lord Nelson" was in charge, a rare sight in Lime Street as it was the first time that a Southern locomotive had been to this famous station. The band of the Staffordshire Regiment entertained before departure, playing the 13-coach special away at 1035. The green Deltic, 55002, officiated with the return train travelling by way of Doncaster, Sheffield, Chinley and the Ashburys-Phillips Park line. *(Tom Heavyside)*

Scarborough Spa Express

In 1981 the BR-sponsored 'Scarborough Spa Express' provided work for a variety of preserved locomotives. On its inaugural run on 23 May maroon-painted Pacific No 46229 *Duchess of Hamilton* was in charge and is seen at York awaiting departure. On 4 August A4 Pacific No 4498 *Sir Nigel Gresley* provided this chance photograph, also taken at York, after arrival with the return morning working. Class 50 No 50040 *Leviathan* was at the head of the customary test train after overhaul and refurbishment at BREL Doncaster. *(Bill Sharman, Brian Cooke)*

Open day visitors

LMS Pacific No 46229 *Duchess of Hamilton* was in Crewe Works for repairs on the occasion of its popular Open Day on 6 June 1981. The previous day, No 46229 presented this once familiar sight as it waits for admirers. *(Barry Nicolle)*

Pride of the GWS, No 5051 is pictured passing under the Golborne Road bridge at Westbourne Park on 20 September, when a shuttle service was operated between Paddington and Old Oak Common to convey visitors to the latter depot's Open Day. The heads hanging out of the windows reveal the direction in which the train is travelling! *(Brian Cooke)*

At the other end of the shuttle was class 9F No 92220, photographed leaving the parcels platform at Paddington with one of the specials. *(Bill Sharman)*

Glasgow Works Open Day, held on 27 June, was another occasion incorporating a steam shuttle service. Two events were commemorated by the Open Day; the 125th anniversaries of both St Rollox Works and of the Glasgow-Garnkirk Railway. The Strathspey Railway provided 'Black Five' No 5025 which is seen leaving for Garnqueen on a shuttle. NBR 0-6-0 *Maude* from the SRPS at Falkirk also officiated on this duty. *(Colin Boocock)*

Black 5s at work

The railway fraternity is renowned for celebrating anniversaries, some a little dubious and perchance an excuse for a little extra publicity! Others are more deserving and 1981 marked several worthy anniversaries. One of these was the 200th anniversary of the birth of George Stephenson. To mark this occasion an exhibition and fair was held at Wylam, the birthplace of this great engineer, and special trains hauled by No 4767 *George Stephenson* ran between Newcastle and Hexham. One of these trains passes Dilston on 6 June 1981. *(Les Nixon)*

The Hull Locomotive Preservation Group's Class 5 No 5305 is noted by BR engineers for its exemplary mechanical condition and by enthusiasts for its external finish. No 5305 gave several faultless runs in 1981 and was one of the locomotives rostered to work the 'Trans-Pennine Pullman' over the highly photogenic Diggle route. The photographic qualities of this line are illustrated in this view of No 5305 on the climb to Standedge tunnel. *(Peter Skelton)*

Earlier in the year, on 28 February, No 4767 provided this fine sight coming south at Ais Gill with SLOA's 'Cumbrian Mountain Express'. (*John Hunt*)

Carnforth-based 'Black 5' No 5407 lifts the season's final BR 'Cumbrian Coast Express' up Lindal bank on 1 September. (*Bill Sharman*)

Old favourites on the Didcot run

On 11 April Ivatt class 4 2-6-0 No 43106 had an outing on the main line when it handled the Dorridge-Didcot-Dorridge portions of SVR Railtours' appropriately named 'Flying Pig' tour from Manchester. The locomotive is seen here passing *Heyford* on the return trip. *(Les Nixon)*

It was good to see 4-6-0 No 7029 *Clun Castle* return to active service on 10 October 1981 with 'The Dinting Venturer'. The southbound train is seen approaching Tackley Halt. *(Peter Skelton)*

Class 9F No 92220 *Evening Star* is no longer *persona non gratis* with BR. It was suspended from main line duties on account of its flangeless driving wheels and the possibility of derailment on raised check rails but is now passed to run between Didcot and Dorridge. The Great Western Society completed an overhaul on the 9F in 1981 and the locomotive presented a fine sight on 13 September 1981 with 'The Rising Star', seen here passing Somerton. Organised by GWS Railtours, the train ran from Paddington to Stratford-on-Avon with steam haulage forward from Didcot. *(Peter Skelton)*

Anniversary Venturer

Two special trains featuring steam haulage were run on 3 October to mark the tenth anniversary of the return to steam haulage on BR. Sponsored by 6000 LA Railtours, the 'Anniversary Venturer' originated from Newton Abbot and was hauled by Castle 4-6-0 No 5051 *Earl Bathurst* from Didcot to Dorridge and, appropriately, by the locomotive which inaugurated the return to steam in 1971, No 6000 *King George V*, over the Shrewsbury-Newport section.

Earl Bathurst is seen here in action near Aynho, while later the same day *KGV* made a fine sight as it threaded the magnificent border countryside near Marshbrook as the 'Anniversary Venturer' made for Newport. *(both: Peter Skelton)*

On 19 June a private charter, 'The Permanent Wayfarer', was run over the Settle & Carlisle line headed by the legendary No 4472 *Flying Scotsman*. Captured on film breasting the summit at Ais Gill on the soutbound leg, the train includes the eight Pullman cars purchased early in 1981 by the Steam Locomotive Operators Association. Being both dual heated and dual braked, these coaches were obtained to ensure a rake of modern stock was available in view of the rapid withdrawal of steam heated, vacuum braked Mk 1 stock. The Pullmans which include seven of the Second Parlours, Nos E347-E353 and M354, formerly the 'Hadrian Bar', are maintained at Carlisle. *(Roger Cruse)*

26 August 1981 saw *Flying Scotsman* officiating on 'The Scarborough Spa Express', one of a wide variety of locomotives utilised on this new service. The A3's graceful lines are in evidence in this view of No 4472 backing onto its train and crossing the River Ouse at York. *(Bill Sharman)*

Other duties for this notable machine included turns on the 'North Yorkshireman' and for the first two weeks that this train operated, the empty coaching stock was stabled in Bradford Forster Square station. Subsequently, the stock was held at Valley Road Goods depot, Bradford, prior to returning to Keighley to resume its homeward run. No 4472 *Flying Scotsman* is seen on this duty at Forster Square on 23 June 1981. *(Les Nixon)*

Scotsman in action

Effortless 'Streaks'

A4 afficionados were given several opportunities during 1981 to see the class in action. On May 9 the ever popular No 60009 *Union of South Africa* was used on the Edinburgh-Perth leg of the SLOA two-day 'North Briton' railtour from London. It is seen here complete with SLOA Pullmans having just passed Blackford crossing, south-west of Gleneagles. *(Bill Sharman)*

No 4498 *Sir Nigel Gresley* takes it easy as its coasts down through Ribblleshead with the southbound 'Cumbrian Mountain Express' on 14 July. The great mass of Whernside dominates the threatened viaduct. *(Les Nixon)*

A two-day tour from England in Scotland using the SLOA Pullman train included in its itinery haulage in tandem by two of the most popular preserved steam locomotives, NBR 0-6-0 No 673 *Maude* and LNER 4-4-0 No 246 *Morayshire*. The pair present a fine sight leaving Larbert on 10 May 1981. *(Colin Boocock)*

The Scottish Region entertained steam traction again on the Highland main line when class 5 No 5025 journeyed to Aviemore — its present home! It is pictured on the return leg of 'The Speyside Express' near Pitlochry on 20 July 1981. *(Roger Cruse)*

Steam north of the border

Welcome return

The North Eastern Locomotive Preservation Group's 2-6-0 K1 No 2005 was back in main line service on 24 October following a major overhaul which included re-tyring the driving wheels. No 2005 doubleheaded with Class 5 No 4767 *George Stephenson* from Middlesbrough to Hellifield via Newcastle and Carlisle, from whence they went light to Carnforth to spend the winter. No 2005 leads No 4767 out of the early morning mist near Billingham crossing. *(Ted Parker)*

One of the most popular preserved locomotives, *Leander*, returned to main line service on 5 December 1981 following boiler overhaul on the Severn Valley Railway. No 5690 returned to its home base at Carnforth by means of a Sheffield-Leeds-Carnforth-Sellafield excursion which was notable in that BR sanctioned for steam operation the section between Normanton (Altofts Junction) to Leeds, thus permitting steam haulage throughout the tour. No 5690 had worked light engine to Butterley from the SVR prior to its outing and was stabled there overnight before proceeding to Sheffield to take up its train. *Leander* is captured on film in beautiful lighting conditions passing Cudworth with the special. With the exception of the leading and rear Mk 1 BCKs, note the absence of heads from the SLOA owned Pullmans. The inability of patrons to savour the sights and aromas from open windows is a heavily criticised feature of the use of these coaches on enthusiasts' specials. *(Les Nixon)*

City of Wells *on the main line*

Newly authorised for main line running on 1981 railtours, Bulleid light Pacific No 34092 *City of Wells* made its first such appearance since restoration on 28 November with the Carnforth-Hellifield leg of the 'Cumbrian Mountain Pullman'. It is seen here near Borwick, shortly after leaving Carnforth. *(Peter Skelton)*

City of Wells was in action again on 12 December with the 'Golden Arrow', creating this fine study as it climbed to Eldroth summit near Clapham against a backdrop of snow-clad fells. It had been intended to run No 34092 through to Leeds but late running of services from the south to connect with the railtour as a result of adverse weather led to reversal of the train at Skipton, with the Pacific making its return run tender first. *(Ted Parker)*